SEVEN QUICK CASH FIXES

FOR ANY BUSINESS IN THE NEXT 30 DAYS

BETSI BIXBY

Seven Quick Cash Fixes: For Any Business in the Next 30 Days

Copyright © 2016 by Betsi Bixby

All rights reserved. No part of this publication may be reproduced, distributed, or transmitted in any form or by any means, including photocopying, recording, or other electronic or mechanical methods, without the prior written permission of the publisher, except in the case of brief quotations embodied in critical reviews and certain other noncommercial uses permitted by copyright law.

Printed in the United States of America

ISBN-13: 978-1495465130

LCCN: 2014911638

www.7quickfixesbook.com

Acclaim For

As a banker, I know the importance of cash flow! In *The Seven Quick Fixes*, Betsi has nailed it. Any business will gain from just doing even one of two of her fixes! Knowing she was a fellow banker and coming from a background of complexity, the thing that amazed me is how easy the book is to follow. Truly practical and inspiring. *-Kent Hudson, Senior Vice President, First Financial Bank, N.A.*

"Your company is profitable, so WHERE IS THE CASH"? Betsi's words during a presentation over 20 years ago began our relationship and she has helped me grow and prosper ever since. Her vast knowledge of business helped put in place a foundation for growth and success, not only in business, but also personally. Brilliant and informative, you won't have to ask: "SHOW ME THE MONEY"!
-Tony Savoie, President/CEO, Richard Oil and Fuel Holding Company, INC; Richard Oil and Fuel, LLC; Popingo's Convenience Stores, LLC; JAS Real Estate, LLC

As a business owner wanting to bless my family, employees and communities we serve, I've thoroughly enjoyed my monthly executive coaching sessions with Betsi so was thrilled to learn she is taking her wisdom to a wider audience through her Seven Quick Cash Fixes. Don't let the simplicity of her message and the easy to follow steps keep you from taking action. She knows her stuff and in this book stresses the often overlooked fundamentals that have big cash impact. Just do it! *-Jerry Westgate, President, Wesco, INC., Wesco chain of convenience stores in the greater half of Michigan*

The title of this book says it all... *The Seven Quick Cash Fixes for Any Business Right Now* is exactly what Betsi delivers in this no nonsense, straight to the point how to manual for any business. Betsi loves business, loves people, loves leadership and had made a better cash position achievable which will bless many. *-David Hoyt, President, John Maxwell Company*
As one of the many family businesses that Betsi has helped, I can tell you everything in The Seven Quick Fixes works! Do exactly what she says and you will have more cash just as promised.
- Wendell Wakefield- Wakefield Oil Co., INC

As the agent who represented Betsi in her first book with Jack Canfield (Soul of Success Volume 2) I am thrilled to see her sharing decades of business experience in *Seven Quick Cash Fixes for Any Business Right Now*. If you have a business, or are even thinking of starting a business, you don't want to miss the secrets she reveals. Success or failure often comes down to one or two things that you understand better than your competitors, this is the one that could put you over the top, don't miss it!
-Nick Nanton, *Emmy Award winning director/producer and agent to celebrity experts*

This book is the answer to cash flow issues that face every business from time to time. More importantly, it lays out exactly what you need to do to never repeat cash flow problems again. A must read for every business owner in America. -Dave Lakhani, *President, Bold Approach, Inc. and author of Persuasion: The Art of Getting What You Want, and Inc. 500 Entrepreneur*

The Seven Quick Fixes reveals a proven framework useful for any business needing to generate more cash quickly. Betsi shows up filled up in her breakthrough book, weaving a masterful model that educates businesses on how to decrease stress and increase their bottom line. Read her words and reap the benefits. —Kary Oberbrunner, *Author of Day Job to Dream Job, The Deeper Path, and Your Secret Name*

Seven Quick Cash Fixes for Any Business Right Now gives managers of small and mid-size businesses practical common sense techniques for improving cash flow and profitability. Betsi Bixby, using her extensive expertise honed by advising over 3,500 companies and clear straightforward language, provides time tested proven methods using real life examples to guide you through the quick fix methods. This book is invaluable reading for business experts and novices alike.
-Dr. Gerald Swanson, *Professor Emeritus of Economics at the University of Arizona and author of America the Broke: How the Reckless Spending of the White House and Congress Are Bankrupting Our Country and Destroying Our Children's Future and Bankruptcy 1995: The Coming Collapse of America and How to Stop It.*

Knowledge and wisdom are two essential components for success and Betsi Bixby has an abundance of both. When I was named PMAA President in 1998, Betsi was overseeing PMAA national benchmarking surveys and I quickly recognized the great resource she was for the petroleum marketing industry. Over the past seventeen years, when I needed to better understand a marketer operations issue, I turned to Betsi and she always had the answer. I was delighted to learn she is now publishing a book, as it will be a great resource for anyone wanting to improve their business. – *Dan Gilligan, President of Petroleum Marketers Association of America from 1998 to 2015*

As CEO of InfusionSoft where we provide sales and marketing software for tens of thousands of small businesses, *The Seven Quick Fixes* is exactly what any business needs that is periodically short on cash. I'm happy to see this book come to fruition as Betsi's mission and passion about family businesses is totally aligned with mine and our growing team at InfusionSoft. It's rewarding for me to see our long-term customer blessing more businesses through this powerful how-to book with simple yet effective steps for any business to have more cash. – *Clate Mask, CEO, Infusionsoft. Serving over 30,000 small businesses.*

Our family business connected with Betsi nearly a decade ago. Her methods have helped us to grow to heights that we only dreamed of before we met Betsi. She introduced us to her quick cash fixes and they set us on a path to double digit growth for 5 years running. - *Bill Gallagher, Managing Director, Offen Petroleum, Inc.*

Every dollar I have spent working with Betsi Bixby and her Meridian staff has been returned to me tenfold. She knows cash and cash flow like the back of her hand and my business is proof! We've considered her and the team our secret weapon for over 15 years. When it came time to make a transition and sell, she was our first and only choice. Believe what she says in The Seven Quick Fixes and do it fast if you want to see your cash grow. -*Bill Rawson, President, Cardwell Distributing, Inc.*

As a rapidly growing multigenerational family company, maintaining a strong cash position as we grow is absolutely necessary. Our team did Betsi's Seven Fixes in our coaching program with her and immediately gained. Every family business needs The Seven Fixes no matter how successful and how fat their cash balance! - *Luc Pepin, CEO, Pepco Corporation*

The Seven Quick Fixes is an incredibly practical book! Betsi's passion for the success of family business shines strong and clear in her words. She has a God-given talent for simplifying complex financial concepts into easy to understand steps. She has lived this, cultivated this and demonstrated this for decades. Her decades of reproducing results through consulting means this book will be blessing for those who follow her sage wisdom! - *Mark Cole, CEO, The John Maxwell Company*

Having interviewed over 6,000 CEOs and hundreds of "celebrity" business consultants, I immediately knew that Betsi was authentic, driven and passionate about helping their businesses. Since meeting back in the 90's, we've had occasion to work together on a few projects. The fact that she is now sharing all her cash flow wisdom in The Seven Quick Fixes is exciting to me and should be even more to you! Her practical advice works!" - *Bob Chesney- Host & Executive Producer, Window on Wall Street TV*

Betsi draws from her experience both in the financial industry and in the small business sector to bring a unique and very simplified look at cash flow. This book is special in the way that it is straightforward. By pulling back the veil of mystique on this often underutilized weapon she is able to help the reader understand how they can use these tools more effectively to allow their business to be more liquid. I think this book will prove to be useful for years to come to both seasoned executives and young entrepreneurs. - *C.A. McConnell, founder of CAM Forge Tools, Inc.*

7 Quick Cash Fixes is a valuable resource for any business owner. Betsi Bixby draws on her extensive experience as a banker turned entrepreneur, offering advice that's practical, proven, and easy to understand. If you're serious about infusing your business with more cash—and who isn't—this book is a gem! - *Dr. Gloria Burgess, Entrepreneur and Best-Selling Author of Legacy Living and Dare to Wear Your Soul on the Outside*

Drawing on decades of business experience, Betsi Bixby has written a most practical and valuable "how-to" guide for business owners and managers who care about the financial health of their organization.
Packed with ideas, examples, and stories, Seven Quick Cash Fixes will get your cash-generating juices flowing. I recommend that you read this book, follow the guidelines, and employ the strategies. Your cash balance will increase, and you'll thank Betsi! - *John E. Burgess, CPA, CMA, CGMA, and Maestro: Music for Transformation*

This book gives every business owner the opportunity to learn from Betsi's goal oriented, no nonsense, strategic approach that she's used to help hundreds of entrepreneurs and family run businesses. I've personally seen her work transform the lives of many teams and individuals and I'm glad she's been able to incorporate many of her teachings and philosophies in this powerful book. In the pages within, you'll find a unique blend of actionable ideas, quick fix tactics, and proven strategies to help your business generate AND keep more cash for your company's financial well-being. -*Tom Latourette, Managing Partner, m3 Learning, Providing sales training to over 300,000 sales professionals.*

A rock solid business book and so much more than 7 Quick Cash Fixes, Betsi Bixby's book is packed with "use it right now guidance" along with web resources including her own email address, a toolkit, chapter action steps and more. Instruction manual, action plan and financial psychology packed into one, Betsi Bixby has created a valuable resource for any business owner to immediately improve their cash position. Sprinkled with the biblical wisdom, Betsi teaches any business owner how to become an even better steward of resources. Betsi guides the reader through a process of measurable goals, focus, and accountability to reach their cash objectives. While positioned as a financial book, the reader is treated to wisdom in leadership, financials, operations, products/services and even marketing. Well done Betsi!!! – *Misty Young, Entrepreneur Extraordinaire known as the Restaurant Lady and author of From Rags to Restaurants*

As owner of a private, international defense company my life revolves around the management of our cash... I love this book! 7 Quick Cash Fixes provides you with some great ideas and tools on how to improve your cash flow. The "Bonus" chapters are filled with detailed explanations, tips, examples and my personal favorite, the WARNINGS. I encourage you to listen to this sound advice about what to watch out for, use the experience being offered to keep from making these mistakes in your business and negatively impacting your cash flow. This book should be required reading for your leadership team!
-Art Barter, President and CEO, Datron World Communications, Inc. and CEO, Servant Leadership Institute, Inc.

In the process of building and being recognized as the leader of one of the best and largest Coaching company by Stevie Award as well as T125 as the number one training company, I am a firm believer in education and training for success. Betsi and I share that love. She and I met through our mutual friend and mentor John C. Maxwell, and desire to create value coupled with her business acumen was immediately evident. With The Seven Quick Fixes, she has hit the nail on the head for any business wanting to improve their actual cash. – *Dianna Kokoszka, CEO of Mega Achievement Productivity Systems (MAPS), leading a team of more than 100 MAPS coaches*

In a money crunch? Short on cash? Need to improve your money flow? In *7 Quick Cash Fixes*, Betsy Bixby offers "7 quick fixes" to move you towards success and good business habits. Whether you're a new business owner just starting out or a seasoned entrepreneur you'll gain valuable insights, actionable steps, and practical principles to strengthen your business. - *Greg and Julie Gorman, LifePlan Facilitators, John Maxwell Coaches and Best-Selling Authors of What I Wish My Mother Had Told Me about Marriage*

Thank You Betsi! This book is so timely for me as a new product I launched didn't do as well as I anticipated. It was quite depressing and I was wondering how we would get out of this cash crunch. Then along came your book! A combination of #3 and #7 are being implemented immediately! *The Seven Quick Fixes* was easy to read and understand, not like most books on this topic which usually make my eyes glaze over. Thank you so much for sharing all your years of experience. I am very grateful and look forward to your future writings." – *Carla McNeil, Social Media Expert and founder of Butterfly Networking*

Back in the early 90's, I called Betsi after reading one of her practical advice articles. My aim was to convince her to become involved with the Texaco association I was running. It worked! Every convention I ran after that call, I invited Betsi to speak and her sessions were always packed year after year. I am thrilled that she is bringing you her cash advice in *The Seven Quick Fixes* since I've witnessed Texaco and Shell branded marketers gain from her wisdom over the years. – *Tom West, Retired National Association of Shell and Texaco Marketers Association Executive*

*Dedicated to my daughter Sheila,
a huge blessing in my life.*

TABLE OF CONTENTS

INTRODUCTION 1

Chapter 1- Essential Questions 7
    Are cash shortages affecting your business and your life? These diagnostics pinpoint the actions that will help you the fastest.

Chapter 2- Fix Cash Fast Success Tips 13
    Are you time-crunched? How to get the most cash out of this book the fastest!

Chapter 3- Quick Fix # 1 17
    Does your company issue credit to customers? A quick cash producer cash that helps a customer clear their conscience while you increase your cash!

Chapter 4- Quick Fix #2 19
    Have you ever heard the phrase, "You never know until you ask"? Here's where we find cash just waiting for you for the asking!

Chapter 5- Quick Fix #3 21
    Does your business include inventory? Then learn how to lighten your load and waste less time while producing a pile of cash.

Chapter 6- Quick Fix #4 25
    Do you buy from vendors? Let them help you increase your cash.

Chapter 7- Quick Fix #5 27
    Do you borrow money? Find out how your banker can help your cash without increasing your debt.

Chapter 8- Quick Fix #6 29
    Have you bought a bunch of stuff? Assets can pile up over time so discover how to increase space and bring in some cash.

Chapter 9- Quick Fix #7 31
    Do you have satisfied customers? Keep them intrigued as they build your bank account.

Chapter 10- Get It All Organized 33
    Review your fixes from Chapters 1 through 9, prioritize, and GO!

Chapter 11- Turbocharge Your Cash Results 35
    Set your goals and track your cash successes.

Chapter 12- (Finale) Take The Next Step 39
    Creating opportunities for more cash never stops. Get plugged in to even more resources for more cash.

SPECIAL BONUSES

Bonus Section I – Super Fast Receivables

Chapter 13	Written Credit Policy	45
Chapter 14	Risk Rating Accounts Receivable	51
Chapter 15	Appropriate Customer Credit Limits.	57
Chapter 16	Super Speedy Collections via 100% EFT. .	63
Chapter 17	Seven Step Plan to Fewer Bad Debts	67

Bonus Section II – Inventory Power

Chapter 18	Reduce Inventory for Higher Profits	73
Chapter 19	Inventory – Do You Have It Yet?.	79
Chapter 20	Automated Inventory Control.	83
Chapter 21	Target Marketing and Replenishment	89
Chapter 22	Inventory Error and Loss Checklist	93

Bonus Section III – Really Smart Banking

Chapter 23	What Are You Worth to Your Bank?	101
Chapter 24	How to Get Your Banker to Yes.	105
Chapter 25	Loan Interest Pricing Options.	109
Chapter 26	Structuring New Financing.	113
Chapter 27	Keep Your Banker Happy.	117
Chapter 28	Help for Tapped Out Bank Credit Lines	121
Chapter 29	When to Switch Banks	127
Chapter 30	Better Banking Checklist.	131

Bonus Section IV – Marketing on Steroids

Chapter 31	How to Keep Profitable Customers	137
Chapter 32	Target Marketing.	141
Chapter 33	Hit the Emotional Hot Button.	147

INTRODUCTION

Cash in your business doesn't create happiness, but it sure makes life easier. All business owners I know want to increase their company's cash. Is that you?

Whether you are reading this book just to "tweak" your cash up a little for growth, or you know first-hand the gut-wrenching feeling of a true cash crunch – no money for payroll, having to fire long-term employees, selling off assets, or even closing down partial operations, this book can help you.

When a business is short on cash repeatedly, owners lose sleep and lose confidence. When the problem persists, it strains marriages, tempers and in worst cases causes divorce or even suicide. Cash shortages effect entire families.

In the skinny margin world I live in, cash isn't a want, it's a need. While strong cash flow is vital to any business; it's the lifeblood of paper-thin margin businesses where gross profits are literally measured in pennies. These skinny margin family businesses are my clients. Their profits are measured in tenths of a cent, not dollars. So they have no room for sloppiness or errors. If they lose money on one deal, it can take them dozens, even scores, of others to recoup their loss.

And I have a confession. Prior to the recession, the techniques in this book while proven, effective and highly practical, weren't personal to me. They were just for my clients. But shortly into the recession, after a vital division in my own company simply dried up from market forces, I suddenly found myself in the cash flow vice having to use these techniques to get my own company back on solid cash ground. They really work!

But let me digress. For over two decades, I've been privileged to help thousands of these family owned distribution companies avoid losses and increase their vital cash flow. I've introduced them to practices that have brought them consistent success. During that time, I've discovered that the techniques used in this specialized industry work just as well for companies in other businesses. That's when I decided to write this book.

This book is to get you started on more cash and fast! With market forces hitting so many companies during and after the recession like a ton of bricks, and experiencing my own cash crunch, I felt compelled to get these quick fixes to business owners. Since these approaches have been so profitable for companies that operate on margins in fractions of pennies, imagine what they will do for a business like yours with margins measured in dollars.

And let me humbly admit right now that in most instances, I am not the inventor of these concepts. Most of what you will read is simply what I've learned from others, and I've added my own twist or two, including a few Biblical principles and scripture. Fortunately, I've learned from the best, the top of the heap, and now I'm delighted to pass that knowledge on to you.

About me
Some folks think cash flow training should come from college courses. My cash flow knowledge didn't come from my MBA in Finance, but was first learned in the nation's premier commercial loan officer training program. Starting fresh out of college in the loan officer's chair, and later rising to the rank of Vice President, the Quick Fix cash flow concepts presented in this book were honed as I analyzed hundreds of businesses.

As my banking career progressed, I became frustrated. Often, I could clearly see why a company was not achieving peak cash flow, but banking practices tied my hands and prohibited me from offering help. When enough frustration built up, the entrepreneur in me grew restless, and thus the seeds for my present company, Meridian Associates, Inc., took root.

Let me also admit to you right now that my involvement in the petroleum industry is purely by chance. I can assure you the thought of advising this industry was not my sandbox dream. Instead, a petroleum marketer happened to wander into my multi-windowed corner bank office looking for a loan to build a bulk plant (combination fuel holding tanks, warehouse and offices) and cardlock (unattended commercial fueling facility for commercial vehicles). I can vividly remember listening to him describe his growth, his needs, and knowing I did not have a clue as to what he was talking about. Yet, all the while, I was nodding my head as if I understood every word. (I don't think that technique is taught in loan officer training but it sure was prevalent during my time in the banking industry.)

Finally, towards the end of his request, the marketer informed me that the best thing about his future site was that it was less than a mile from the "rack," I was finally forced to admit my ignorance. I'm not sure your definition of rack, but what I envisioned was certainly not a big fuel terminal where he would pick up product.

A week after I closed the loan for this bulk plant and cardlock, a full year after he first walked in my office, the marketer asked me for dinner date. I agreed and as we developed a relationship, I learned just *how* ignorant I was about petroleum, and he learned how much he didn't know about cash flow. Oh yes, in case you're worried about my ethics, I passed his account off to another loan officer.

As it turned out, his business was growing like a weed. It was very profitable, but broke — always out of cash and borrowing more and more. Each month, he would show me his financial statements, looking for compliments on his profits, only to hear my complaints about his lack of cash. Then, after about six months diligently working on his cash flow, the picture dramatically changed: he began paying down debt plus, he had money in the bank. Life was good.

At about that same time, he became president of an industry trade association, and decided to hold a seminar for his fellow marketers on cash flow. At that time (early1991), bankers were disenchanted with the petroleum industry and reasonably priced bank debt was tough to get and keep. I presented my "Banker's Method of Cash Flow" talk to a group of about 125 petroleum marketers, who had annual sales between $2 million and $500 million, and cash flow that ranged from tight to severely tight. In my closing remarks, I invited them to call me if they needed help with cash flow or financing. That was a Saturday.

Monday morning, my phone at the bank began ringing, and the seeds for Meridian Associates, Inc. started bursting out of the ground. Since that first seminar, I've lost count of the actual number of petroleum distribution companies I've been blessed to help, but it's well over 3,500 companies.

Practical and tested
Now, I've read all sorts of business books that promise you the stars and moon. Then, when you read them they're confusing, impractical, or overly complex. Many offer vague, untested theories that leave you frustrated or perplexed.

This book is different; it has been designed for your success. You don't have to be a financial guru to read it because it's written in simple, straightforward language so those with no financial training can still grasp and use the concepts. To make it even easier to understand and retain, you'll find lots of common sense and real life examples sprinkled throughout its pages.

The techniques in this book are not academic or theoretical—they're time-tested, proven methods that will boost your cash as well as your profits. And they will work for virtually all types of businesses, if you act. Make no mistake though; you cannot achieve the success you crave without taking action. While all of the ideas in this book really work, and fast, they take effort and some persistence. (I'm reminded of James 1:22, "Be doers of the word" God likes action too!) If you apply these quick fix lessons of the tough distribution industry to your business, you can indeed begin making serious improvements in your cash.

How to use this book
To get the most from this book, read and complete the first two chapters. Then, you can turn to any of the other chapters and feel free to proceed at your own speed and in any order you wish.

Chapter One is the foundation of this book. Read it first because it lays the groundwork for the material covered in the chapters that follow. Let me explain why completing this first chapter is so important.

Chapter One, Essential Questions, requires you to examine the actual problems your cash shortage has caused. It's crucial for you to identify your precise problems, to understand them and their implications so you know what to address. This is the diagnostic stage: unless you know, up front, precisely where you need help, you can end up wasting your valuable time on solutions that won't work.

Chapter Two will tell you how to use this book to get cash the fastest. The next seven chapters, the Seven Quick Fixes, are designed to give you that quick start — to infuse your business with a fast and easy cash boost that you will immediately see and feel. In business, success is a cumulative, long-term process that is built on repeated successes. These quick fixes will get you started. They are intended to prime the pump, to get success flowing. Your initial successes will encourage you to continue moving forward direction and help you form good business habits.

The Bonus Chapters are a sneak preview to my next book. In the Bonus Chapters you'll move on to techniques that may take a bit more time and diligence to complete. Such as how to transition from a receivables based company to virtually all cash, or how to seriously reduce inventory while increasing your profits through non-traditional, counterintuitive techniques. You have lots to look forward to!

But for right now, as you proceed with the 7 Quick Fixes, you may be able to jump right into several of them at one time. Or you may find that not all necessarily apply to your particular business. For instance, if you're in retail, you probably don't have receivables. So, just skip material that doesn't apply to you.

Each chapter includes a step-by-step action plan, with a space for you to write the date you began, the date you completed the action, and your cash savings. A space has also been provided to insert the name of the person accountable for implementing that step. Be sure to enter the beginning and ending dates, even if you delegate any actions to others, because those dates will keep you on track and give you a sense of accomplishment.

For your convenience, and particularly if you'll be working the action plans with your staff, all the action plans plus cool calculator tools and other bonuses are available for download at www.7QuickFixesBook.com. Just click on "Quick Fixes Toolkit."

As you experience cash success, please share it with me at that site. You'll find your success story could be worth even more cash as we'll be rewarding outstanding successes! While there, click onto the info button for our inexpensive webinar-based business coaching that has blessed participants with amazing cash results.

If prior to reading this book, you already mastered any of the actions that I recommend, excellent, good for you. Either review those portions again or just skip them and read on until you've completed everything else of interest to you.

Enjoy this book and refer to it often. If you have questions or comments, please email them to me at betsi@7QuickFixesBook.com. Now, let's get going; start building up your business and your bank account.
~Betsi Bixby

> ***Phil 4:13 I can do all things through God who strengthens me.***

P.S. Did scripture in a business book surprise you? Whether you are a person of faith or not, the business principles will work! After years of personally ignoring God, I am now firmly convinced that He is the true author of success and wants us blessing our families and scores of others through our businesses. I hope my breaking the "business book mold" with inclusion of Bible verses will not offend you and at best bless you. Maybe they will even confirm your faith in your business, confirm that your business, your daily work, can be your true calling and ministry as it is for me.

> ***Col 3:23 And whatever you do, do it heartily, as to the Lord and not to men.***

Chapter 1

ESSENTIAL QUESTIONS

Do you want more cash in your business? Have you had months when your business was profitable, but it felt like it wasn't, that it was flat out broke because the cash ran out? Do you want more cash so you can:

- Meet your expenses more easily to pay suppliers, payroll, or taxes?
- Purchase equipment to be more efficient and grow?
- Expand?
- Get out of or reduce debt?
- Look good on financial statements so you can get lower loan interest rates or higher credit lines?

If you answered yes to any of those questions, then let me tell you a true story about a distributor that used the methods in this book to get serious about cash. When the distributor came to me, it was close to the end of its third quarter. Because of high growth and lack of knowledge or training in cash flow, in less than nine months the company had eaten through $495,313 of its precious cash since its last year-end. It hadn't meant to do it, it just sort of happened as the company was growing. The operation was very profitable, but going broke.

Everyone at the company was feeling the stress. On the days when big payments were due like payroll or large supplier or tax payments, it was no fun. The owner was even afraid to tell his wife that things were that tight. She was still spending and using charge cards like everything was fine. After all, the company was very profitable!

The stress caused the owner to reach out to me. By using the techniques you are going to learn in this book, in just three months, this owner helped the company generate $1,029,074 in cash, erasing its year-to-date deficit and generating even more cash. How? By getting serious. The owner and his team diligently used all 7 methods in this book to change their cash position by their year-end.

With a big fat cash balance of $1,408,536 on its year-end statement, good things began to happen. First, the company was able to stop borrowing on its bank line of credit. With the good-looking fiscal year-end financial statement showing that big cash balance, the owner negotiated lower interest rates on new equipment loans needed the following year. Finally, the company was able to increase its major supplier credit limits, which before the increase were beginning to constrict its growth. For distributorships, this is vital because if you can't get more product, you can't grow.

They work

It doesn't matter how big or small your company is, what type of business you're in, the amount of your cash right now, or even if you don't have any — the techniques in this book work. I've now helped over three thousand companies to increase their cash. They've done it, and, I know you can too — if you are willing to act.

Find what's wrong

Before you attempt to fix your problems, you must know precisely what those problems are and the full impact they have on your present cash position and on your company. So let's take a little time to identify what's been plaguing you and some of the specific harm they've caused so we know exactly what to attack.

NOTE: If you're a "A" type personality like most of my clients and are tempted to skip right over these three questions — don't! Answer them fully. Completing all of these questions is vital; it's too important to omit. It's not necessary to write a long essay on each, but try to give full and well-thought-out answers.

Get a pen and fill in the following blanks. This Chapter 1 worksheet and a bunch of neat tools are also available at www.7QuickFixesBook.com by clicking on "Quick Fix Toolkit."

1. First, examine affects of your cash shortage on your business. Is it preventing your company from meeting payroll, paying suppliers, or expanding? Is it causing you to work too long or hard?

On the lines below, fill in the all of the problems your lack of cash is having on just your business.

Not having enough cash in my business is causing the following business problems:

- _____
- _____
- _____
- _____
- _____

2. In most instances, I find that a company's lack of cash spills over into its owners and operators' personal lives; it has a PERSONAL impact. Your company's cash problems might have you working longer hours, spending less time with your family, not feeling well, straining your marriage or not taking the vacations you dreamed about a few years ago.

On the lines below, write in the personal impact that your businesses' cash shortage has had on you, your life, and the people you love.

Not having enough cash in my business is causing these personal impacts:

- _____
- _____
- _____
- _____
- _____

3. Finally, how would your life be different if you solved your business' cash problems? Would your work schedule change? Would your lifestyle change? Let yourself dream a little, and list what you would do if your company were flush with cash:

If my company had ample cash, I would:

- _____
- _____
- _____
- _____
- _____

Good work. Pat yourself on the back for taking the first step. The fact that you completed these exercises shows me that you're serious about changing your cash position.

> Keep these lists and your answers. Read them from time to time to check whether you're still on track.
>
> Put these questions and your answers in a place where you can easily get to and refer to them. Read them over from time to time. If you find yourself getting off track or find that your cash projects have somehow landed on the back burner:
>
> - ❑ Go back and review these lists.
> - ❑ Think about your answers.
> - ❑ Examine how you implemented them.
> - ❑ Identify what went wrong.
> - ❑ Then, start again.

Action items

- Answer the essential cash flow questions.
- List the major problems you found.
- See which problems you can immediately solve and how you can solve them.
- Fill in the *7 Quick Cash Flow Fixes* Success Tracker below:

Keeping track of progress in your business is key to staying motivated, for you and your employees. Since this is the Quick Fix book, the tracking is boiled down to only the most essential elements -- what, when, how much and who. Each chapter, fill out your Success Tracker. Why? Because companies that <u>measure and track</u> are those that succeed the fastest!

7 Quick Fixes Cash Success Tracker

Actions to Take	Start Date	Finished	Cash Produced	Person Responsible

2 Cor. 9:8 And God is able to make all grace abound toward you, that you, always having sufficiency in all things, may have an abundance for every good work.

Chapter 2

FIX CASH FAST SUCCESS TIPS

If you're like most business owners, you want more cash in your account, and you want it right now, not in six months.

I remember my first cash crunch vividly. After soaring successfully for many years, I decided to make a serious business expansion. It entailed buying a new office, and doubling my staffing. What I didn't see coming was an economic change that would literally dry up 75% of my company's revenues. I know the heartburn, disappointment and anxiety of a cash flow crunch! So, without delay, I'm going explain exactly what you should do.

I've specifically chosen seven quick cash producers that will immediately put money in your coffers and turbocharge your success. All of these cash producers really work; they're time tested, tried and true. In addition to bringing in the cash fast, they will get you thinking about other income sources you can tap.

In some instances, only a single phone call could be standing between you and more cash. One call could land you $10,000 or even $100,000, but in the beginning, it usually pays to start on a smaller scale. When you start small, feel your way along, learn what to do and what to avoid, get all the steps down pat, enjoy small cash successes, then build on them.

Look at your first successes as small jewels that will lead you deeper into the mine where the big diamonds are buried. First, scoop up tiny little fragments. Then, dig deeper into this book where you will find a series of instructions that show you how to obtain bigger chunks of cash. As you proceed, remember that you'll be learning a cumulative process that builds step by step. So learn these early lessons well because you'll be building on them. Also keep in mind that the greater your efforts, the greater your cash rewards.

So, let's get started with my seven quick cash producers. As you read the following chapters, here is what you should do:

- ☐ Check off each cash producer that will work for <u>your</u> business.
- ☐ Estimate how quickly each cash producer could work for you.
- ☐ Prioritize the cash producers you've selected according to how <u>quickly</u> they will work for you; listing the quickest first and so on.
- ☐ Start with prioritized cash producer number one. The faster you jump into action, the faster you'll have more cash!
- ☐ When you complete cash producer number one, proceed to cash producer number two.
- ☐ Use all the cash producers until you've collected all available cash.
- ☐ Watch your cash grow and record your gains in the *7 Quick Fixes Success Tracker* that I've included at the end of each chapter.

> **NOTE:** You may be tempted to go right to the biggest dollar cash producer. Don't! Trust me on this! Do the fastest first!

UPS AND DOWNS

One of the things I love about business and cash flow success is that it's a journey, an adventure. As the days, weeks, months, and years roll by, it always seems to have its ups and downs.

A client just contacted me to let me know the company just landed a big contract that will double its sales. He knew that to properly make this big jump, it will be essential to keep a careful eye on cash flow. He wanted to thank me for the techniques that are now so well ingrained and strong cash-supporting systems and procedures already in place.

His call made me confident his company will absorb all the new growth with minimal "bad" cash days. That should also be your ambition: to get beyond "bad" cash days and keep all those dollars rolling in.

> *James 1:2 My brethren, count it all joy when you fall into various trials, knowing that the testing of your faith produces patience.*

Chapter 3

QUICK FIX #1

Collect <u>one</u> old receivable or prior bad debt.

If you run a business that has receivables, one of the quickest, easiest ways to produce cash is by collecting an old write-off. The account could still be active in your receivables, or one that cost you cash long ago and may be long forgotten.

Do you know that not being able to pay a bill can eat at an honest man's conscience for years? One of my clients had written off a farmer's account when a bad year made the farmer go belly up. When the farmer got back on his feet and started up business again, he went to a different supplier. My client figured it was because of the farmer's embarrassment.

He decided to call the farmer as he'd heard he was now doing well. Much to his surprise, the farmer took his call and proceeded to say how badly he had felt for years about that debt, how he now had the cash, and could he "write him a check?" What a blessing for both parties and now the farmer is buying from him again.

Even though time has passed, you'll be amazed at how much you can collect, especially when your customer's circumstances have changed.

Delegate this task to a trusted employee, a collection agency, a debt negotiator, or even your attorney. Or, pick up the phone yourself. What is most important is that YOU decide which account is most likely to be collectible and then be sure to try to collect on it. Take action!

TIP: If you delegate the effort to an outside professional or internal staff member, check daily on their progress. Make sure they know that you're serious about collecting on this account and that you hand-selected it. Since you're pursuing this account to get a quick fix, pick the target that is most likely to pay you right now. Then, you can move on to the tougher and bigger ones later.

> **NOTE:** When your receivables are for large dollar amounts (check your last balance sheet for the exact figures), go directly to the Bonus Chapter 11, Super Fast Receivables, but first finish reading these quick fixes. In the bonus chapter, you'll learn how to reduce your future slow paying accounts.

Quick Fix #1 Cash Success Tracker

Action	Start Date	Target Finish	Est. Cash	Person Responsible

(If no receivables in your business, leave blank and move on to next chapter)

Chapter 4

QUICK FIX #2

Ask for return of a cash deposit

In the early years, before a company has established a good credit record, landlords, utility companies, vendors, insurance companies, and others often require it to post deposits. As time goes by, it's easy to forget about those deposits. Review your records. Do you have any deposits out there? If so, call and find out if you're entitled to have your deposit, or a portion of it, returned. Again, only one phone call could be standing between you and your money.

TIP: Question all deposit requests and if you can't avoid them, try to negotiate them down. Then, retrieve them as soon as possible.

SUCCESS FROM ASKING

For over 20 years, one of my clients had a deposit sitting with his main supplier. Finally, at my urging, he made a phone call. The supplier said maybe and asked the company to fax their current financial statements.

Within one week they had their $300,000. Why had the supplier not returned his money earlier? Because my client didn't ask. Why didn't he ask? Because he thought that was just part of doing business, their rule. Seeing the $300,000 deposit on my client's balance sheet was so normal to everyone in the organization that no one in the company ever even questioned it!

Quick Fix #2 Cash Success Tracker

Action	Start Date	Target Finish	Est. Cash	Person Responsible

(If no deposits outstanding in your business,
leave blank and move on to next chapter)

Chapter 5

QUICK FIX #3

Get rid of just one non-turning or slow inventory item.

Return just one unsellable or unprofitable product to the original vendor for cash rebates or credits to your account. If the vendor won't accept returns, sell the item on the open market. Somebody, somewhere will want it.

Get the word out about the sale; post it on eBay. Try marking the item's price down, or group it with another product. For instance, if buyers purchase two high margin items of your choice, give them a bonus item at no additional cost — something you want to get rid of.

Removed from the actual inventory in your organization? Ask your warehouse manager what is the one thing that has been sitting around forever that they'd love to be rid of. No warehouse manager? Check out an inventory turn report. No inventory report? Check out the story on this page! You don't need fancy reports or lots of employees to figure out this cash producer.

I want to stress again that you are looking for Quick Fixes! There will be time later to dig deeper into inventory problems or inefficiencies. Don't get sidetracked from your mission – quick cash! Go through all seven quick fixes, then you can go back and dig for the big diamonds!

FOUND CASH

As part of an acquisition, one of my clients received an old warehouse. The place was a mess and he pretty much avoided even stepping inside.

But, after coming to one of our events when he learned how much his inventory was costing, he promptly toured the warehouse and noted its contents: what was moving, and what was not (he said he could tell by the dust!) Then, in less than three weeks, he sold more than $30,000 worth of goods from the warehouse. Not only did he bring in a nice piece of cash, he gained a cleaner, more organized warehouse.

If inventory is a problem for your company, as soon as you finish all seven Quick Fixes, turn to Bonus Section II for Inventory Power Management. Inventory is expensive; every dollar you sink into it costs you loan interest (or forfeit savings), maintenance, and the counting costs to keep on hand. That can add up and eat into hard-won, precious profit.

Use the Success Tracker to track your Inventory Quick Fix cash success. If you are like most of my clients, your first success will just be the tip of the iceberg.

Quick Fix #3 Cash Success Tracker

Action	Start Date	Target Finish	Est. Cash	Person Responsible

(If your business operates without inventory, leave blank and move on to next chapter)

MONEY MAKER BONUS

Here's a great rule of thumb for inventory. Determine your cost for the goods you sold last month by product. You'll take that product's cost, and divide it by 30 days. The figure you come up with will be the dollar amount of one day's average cost for that one product. Let's say for a particular product you sell daily, the average cost for one day is $500. Then, never stock more days'-worth-of-product than 1.5 times your supplier's delivery frequency. This means that if your supplier delivers once per week, you would never want more than supplier timing (7days) times 1.5 which in this case equals 11.5 days. To translate that to inventory, multiply one day's cost of goods sold ($500) by the 11.5 day for a total of $5,750 in total inventory. Never buy or stock more than 1.5 times the delivery frequency of any product.

NOTE: This formula is for retail goods, finished goods only, not manufacturers. Do not use it for raw materials or work in progress, which will vary based on your manufacturing cycle, suppliers and lead-time.

John 15:2 Every branch in Me that does not bear fruit He takes away, and every branch that bears fruit He prunes, that it may bear more fruit.

Chapter 6

QUICK FIX #4

Pay one key supplier more slowly.

Vendor terms are like interest-free loans — the longer you have to pay, the better. Many vendors will negotiate terms, *but only if you ask*. If you've been a stellar account for a major supplier, ask for extended terms. If your supplier won't budge, seek out alternative suppliers who offer goods of similar quality and will give you longer or better terms. Check the Internet for alternate sources; it can make researching suppliers quick and easy.

If you have no other supply options, consider paying for items with a non-interest bearing credit card. Paying by credit card can provide you with the added bonus of airline miles or rebates.

WARNING: Be careful about paying with credit cards. Do it rarely and only as a temporary fix to increase your cash in a particular month. Whenever you charge a purchase on a non-interest bearing credit card, know with certainty that you can pay the entire bill the following month or you can run up more debt. And that additional debt often carries higher interest rates.

Remember, don't begin with the impossible one! Make a list of possible suppliers and select one or two where you feel you have a small chance. Also consider WHO the right person is to make the call. If you know your negotiation skills are not as good as someone else on staff, it's fine to delegate. Record your supplier action plans on the next page.

Quick Fix #4 Cash Success Tracker

Action	Start Date	Target Finish	Est. Cash	Person Responsible

(If no suppliers or vendors, leave blank and move on to next chapter)

SUPPLIER OFFERS EVEN MORE!

One of our coaching clients, despite being skeptical about getting any supplier to change, called a main supplier and asked for 30-day payment terms (they were at standard 15 days). Not only did the supplier immediately say yes, but when reviewing their account, noticed my client wasn't receiving cigarette volume discounts. (The client had grown their business substantially since the original account set up.)

The next week, that supplier <u>offered</u> a 5-cent per pack rebate! Can you imagine the profit? My client was deliriously happy!

Eph 3:20-21 Now to Him who is able to do exceedingly abundantly above all that we ask or think, according to the power that works in us, to Him be glory in the church by Christ Jesus to all generations, forever and ever. Amen.

Chapter 7

QUICK FIX #5

Call your banker for a lower interest rate.

If you're not used to dealing with bankers, asking for interest rate reductions can be intimidating. But trust me, it works. Most businesses have a number of small loans for their vehicles, equipment and other expenses; it's a standard part of doing business.

So, call your banker. Ask if he or she hates having to process all those little, individual payments as much as you do, and question whether he or she finds it cost effective. See about getting all those little loans consolidated into one big note, and when you do, request an interest rate reduction.

TIP: And while you're at it, call your credit card companies to request reductions in your existing rates.

By the way, if you don't owe anyone, congratulate yourself and move on to the next chapter. Debt free is God's model. If you are still in debt, remember to complete your action plan on the next page.

ONE SHORT PHONE CALL NETS ½%

In one five-minute call to her banker, a client of mine got the interest rate on her existing loan reduced by ½ % on the spot. Later, when she used the techniques you'll learn in the Bonus Section III, Really Smart Banking, she negotiated another full point reduction. With total loans over $7 million, she saved her company a little over $100,000 in annual interest. Yahoo!

Quick Fix #5 Cash Success Tracker

Action	Start Date	Target Finish	Est. Cash	Person Responsible

(If you don't borrow money or have a credit card balance, leave blank and move on to next chapter)

Romans 13:8 Owe no one anything except to love one another.

Chapter 8

QUICK FIX #6

Sell one unused asset.

We all have items we no longer use. They can range from anything as small as an extra computer to as big as a real estate parcel that isn't appreciating as much as we hoped it would. The sad fact is that most businesses have all sorts of stuff lying around that is not being used. Check with your team, take inventory, and figure out what you don't need. Then get rid of it in the most cost-effective manner to produce cash.

Some of the techniques you can use to convert assets into cash include telling your business associates, colleagues, employees, subcontractors, vendors and suppliers. Place classified ads in local publications, newsletters and blogs; put up for-sale signs at your business and other places; list property with agents; and use Internet sites.

TIP: Want to have a little fun? See if one of your employees will try to sell your company's unused items for a part of the purchase price. Offer the employee enough of a commission to give him or her strong incentive to work hard. Using this technique will not only bring in extra cash, but it will make an employee very happy to boot. It will also encourage your other employees to identify and volunteer to sell additional dispensable items.

Remember to fill in your Success Tracker!

Quick Fix #6 Cash Success Tracker

Action	Start Date	Target Finish	Est. Cash	Person Responsible

(If you don't own anything in your business, then think about personal assets that can be converted to cash and then inject that cash into your business!)

PARKED JUNKER TRUCK NETS $4,000!

A client had an old tanker truck parked in his field that hadn't moved for years. Right after being challenged to sell an unused asset, he remembered a customer was looking for a tank about the size of the one on the truck. The customer bought the old truck with the still good tank and had it hauled to his site. A win-win! You never know where you have hidden cash.

Chapter 9

QUICK FIX #7

*Create an irresistible offer
for existing customers.*

When you need cash fast, no one is more likely to buy from you than your satisfied customers. The cheapest way to contact them is by email. (If you don't have email addresses for your customer base, you'll have to resort to alternative methods.) If your offer to your customers is special, something they would be nuts to refuse, it will work every time. Offer only items that they will pay for on the spot because you don't want to end up with receivables, especially from your present customers.

To make your proposition more attractive, offer your existing customers bonuses. Give them items from your inventory, services, or freebies from your suppliers or other businesses that would like to join you in a promotion that your customers would value. For instance, you could offer buyers of your items a free lunch at your friend's restaurant or a gift certificate for a free car wash. Just think about goods or services your customers would want and then call business owners who could supply them.

Also compile a list of items that you can get free that your customers would value. The more bonuses you can offer, the better. Make sure your bonuses are enticing to your customers and that they don't conflict with your offer.

If you don't have email, shame on you, but it's not a problem. Simply use whatever means you have to reach your existing customers. This could be postal mail, faxes, your or other newsletters, fliers or signs.

NOTE: One word of caution about selling to your existing customers. Disclose everything you know about the items: all defects, problems and use limitations. Also be prepared to stand behind goods if they don't work or break down because you don't want to risk losing or alienating a valued customer as a result of the sale.

Quick Fix #7 Cash Success Tracker

Action	Start Date	Target Finish	Est. Cash	Person Responsible

(Don't skip this quick fix! It may be a little more difficult than some the other six quick fixes, but can reap big cash rewards!)

Chapter 10

GET IT ALL ORGANIZED

You've just completed your first brush at your quick fixes so you may have a long list of possible actions from just the seven quick fix chapters. Now you're going to get organized so that you increase cash as absolutely fast as possible. Here's what you'll do:

<u>Action items</u>

- Review ALL your action items from the seven quick fix trackers.
- Prioritize (number) those cash producers according to how quickly they can be accomplished.
- Enter them by start date order on the next page.
- Don't read further until you have completed at least one quick cash-producer.
- As soon as you complete your first quick fix, track your success by filling in date in the "Finished" column.

Congratulations! You've just learned how to begin your cash journey. You've just planted the first seeds and now it's time to nurture them so they can grow and increase your company's cash position. To make sure they continue to grow quickly, read the next chapter -- Supercharge via Measurable Goals and Accountability. After that, you're fully ready to tackle the more involved cash producing techniques that follow in the Bonus Chapters.

Quick Fix Cash Success Tracker

Action Taken	Start Date	Finish Date	Actual Cash	Person Responsible

Total Cash Produced $_____

Congratulations on your cash success!
Want more?

Visit www.7QuickFixesBook.com/coaching
To learn about our affordable one year, 12 sessions, proven cash flow coaching program!

Chapter 11

TURBOCHARGE YOUR CASH RESULTS

Measurable Goals and Accountability

Over the years working with clients, I've studied what segregates moderately successful companies from super successful ones and have come to the conclusion that beyond vision, it boils down to two concepts:

1) Measurable Goals
2) Accountability

Where the importance of these two concepts was driven home for me was at our live seminar events. Several times a year, we bring company owners and key personnel together to learn cash flow concepts that can drive their companies to the next level of success. Because we guarantee our program will produce $100,000 in actionable ideas, we track the dollar value gained by each participant and make sure they have a viable written action plan in place before leaving the event.

Measurement Equals Success

As I would roam the tables checking action plans, I noticed that my already highly successful, high profit companies were excellent at setting measurable goals, while less successful companies would describe goals in such generic terms that neither I or they could know what exactly was expected. For example, a successful company might have on their action plan, "We will reduce Accounts Receivable Days Sales Outstanding by 5 days no later than December 31." The less successful company might express the same idea as, "We will reduce accounts receivable." No quantifiable measure! Interesting!

So, as you go through the Bonus Sections of remaining techniques in this book, there will be more options and I will ask you to set goals. For a goal to be acceptable, it must be **measurable and specific**. The neat thing about having measurable goals is that they provide targets for focus. You'll be amazed at what you and your teams can do when they have clear focus and a target!

You'll also be creating action plans in each chapter. Each action plan should have detailed steps, timeline and person accountable for each step. That brings me to the second differentiator of highly successful companies. In high functioning companies, people are held accountable for agreed upon results.

To make your company into a higher cash-producing machine requires accountability. As owner, the best thing you can do to reinforce accountability is a combination of rewards <u>and</u> consequences. If you are anything like me, you love giving rewards – that's the fun part. But, consequences? Ouch! Well, you need to have consequences too.

After all, if someone ignores your directive or consistently fails to meet expectations or deadlines, shouldn't something happen other than a verbal reminder? (Which, by the way, is usually totally ineffective!) So, accountability means coming up with consequences. Different consequences work with different employees. Depending on whether they value time, money, perks, appreciation, special benefits, etc., whatever they value most is how you instill consequences.

As you go through the remaining chapters, your action plan will include a space for rewards and consequences that would be used with the person responsible at each step.

Selecting rewards

Effective rewards are not always monetary. Rewards can be simple recognition, a celebration and high fives, or even getting to keep a job! You might ask each person or team how they prefer being rewarded.

TIP: I've found rewards that include an employee's spouse and or family are the most highly effective.

Selecting consequences

If you are an entrepreneur, you may have a hard time understanding why you need consequences because you are so intrinsically motivated. So here's the reality check – *not everyone is like you and if mediocre performance is tolerated, it will proliferate.* You must insist on quality performance and be prepared with fairly applied consequences. Again, know what motivates your team. Would having to do an extra project or miss a fun outing, or in dire cases, be sent home, get attention? Your organization is only as strong as its weakest link so don't you be the weak link! Insist on consequences!

FINALE

TAKE THE NEXT STEP

In the best companies, pursuit of additional cash and profit never ends. As a company grows and changes through various economic and business cycles, cash needs change. Growth necessitates more cash!

More Cash and Profit

Wanting to help my own clients maximize cash and profit, and yet knowing that my personal time was limited, in 2006 I created a webinar-based coaching program to lead companies step by step to strategic breakthroughs. I knew most companies were already doing everything they knew how to do to create more cash and profit. But, it was what they didn't know -- what they wouldn't even think to pursue -- that they needed most.

The next hurdle was to figure out a vehicle that worked. I didn't want travel costs for them or me. And, it had to be hugely cost effective. With these criteria in mind, I selected webinars for the format where they could discover what they needed from the comfort of their office, with as many or as little staff as they choose. We launched with 25 brave, trusting companies.

I must admit to you that I held my breath through that entire first class. Questions ran rampant in my mind. Would they "get it," or do their homework, or do the quick sampling I wanted them to do after each session to see if they had cash or profit opportunity? And if they did the sampling, and discovered their Achilles Heels, would they then put their shoulder to the grindstone and make the painful changes? (Change is always painful!)

Quite frankly, that first class didn't just pleasantly surprise me, but outright stunned me with the magnitude of some of their gains. My big winner was a company that negotiated a fuel contract and new terms with several suppliers that ended up putting more than $1.4 million back into their cash! And my very smallest company, a husband and wife team with just a couple of employees, managed to refinance their debt and expand their operations with an acquisition! These are just two examples, but I was thoroughly pumped up by everyone's results.

It takes hard work

The good news is that this coaching program is now available to every business at our www.7QuickFixesBook.com website. However, not everyone is willing to put in the work it takes to drive a company's cash and profits to new levels. Allow me to share what it takes to be successful so you don't waste your time or money.

- **Sincere desire to be better.** If you think you already have all the answers, our program is not for you.
- **Time Commitment.** The actual computer-based instruction sessions are max 90 minutes per session, one session per month, but to drive up cash and profit takes homework -- about 4 hours each month doing sampling for possible cash gains and then more time when you hit something you need to change. How much total time? I can't tell you that because I don't know. It could be from a few hours to a massive project. You'll learn to check Return on Investment, of both staff time and money, before you proceed with any project.
- **Persistence.** Once we help a company discover an opportunity area, it could take months to get it humming along. Our biggest winners were companies who kept plugging away at seemingly impossible tasks until they conquered!
- **Investment.** We purposely enhanced the program and increased the program fee with each new class with an interesting result – the larger the fee the more serious the participant and more importantly, the bigger cash and profits results. And this was with all different size companies from very small operations with just a handful of staff to our giants. The good news for you is this same program is available on demand at our website at literally a fraction of what our clients paid.

- **A Competitive Nature.** We like to give prizes for all sorts of wins, and we noticed our biggest cash and profit winners love to be at the top and recognized. We measure cash results as a percent of total assets and profit gains as a percent as well which means no matter how small your company, you are on a level playing field! This allows us to reward companies for their effort regardless of their asset size or annual sales revenue.

A webinar-based coaching program isn't for everyone, but it's a possible next step if you are serious about driving up your businesses cash and profit. If you haven't joined the program already, go right now to the website and click on the coaching link if you'd like to learn more. I'd love to have your company's cash and profit success story in my next book!

Finally, what you do and how you do it is your opportunity to leave a legacy. I pray that the legacy you leave will be exactly what you dreamed. May God bless you richly.

> *Hebrews `12:1-2 Therefore we also, since we are surrounded by so great a cloud of witnesses, let us lay aside every weight, and the sin which so easily ensnares us, and let us run with endurance the race that is set before us, looking unto Jesus, the author and finisher of our faith, who for the joy that was set before Him endured the cross, despising the shame, and has sat down at the right hand of the throne of God.*

Bonus Chapters

Bonus Section I - Super Fast Receivables
Chapter 13   Written Credit Policy
Chapter 14   Risk Rating Accounts Receivable
Chapter 15   Appropriate Customer Credit Limits
Chapter 16   Super Speedy Collections via 100% EFT
Chapter 17   Seven Step Plan to Fewer Bad Debts

Bonus Section II - Inventory Power
Chapter 18   Reduce Inventory for Higher Profits
Chapter 19   Inventory – Do You Have It Right Yet?
Chapter 20   Automated Inventory Control
Chapter 21   Target Market and Replenishment
Chapter 22   Inventory Error and Loss Checklist

Bonus Section III - Really Smart Banking
Chapter 23   What Are You Worth to Your Bank?
Chapter 24   How to Get Your Banker to Yes
Chapter 25   Loan Interest Pricing Options
Chapter 26   Structuring New Financing
Chapter 27   Keep Your Banker Happy
Chapter 28   Help for Tapped Out Bank Credit Lines
Chapter 29   When to Switch Banks
Chapter 30   Better Banking Checklist

Bonus Section IV - Marketing on Steroids
Chapter 31   How To Keep Profitable Customers
Chapter 32   Target Marketing
Chapter 33   Hit the Emotional Hot Button

Bonus Section I

SUPER FAST RECEIVABLES

You've come to this bonus section because you have serious amounts of cash tied up in accounts receivable. That's <u>your</u> money out there! And you want to get even more serious about getting it in the door faster. This is where you will need to dig in. It will take work.

The first thing is to understand the magnitude of your potential extra profit from faster receivables. There is a calculator in the Quick Fix Toolbox, but you can also do this manually using the following steps:

1) Determine the dollar amount of one day's average receivables sales.
2) Divide your receivables by the one day's sales. This equals your average collection time of Days Sales Outstanding.
3) Compare your DSO to your terms. For example, if your DSO equals 45 days and your terms are 30 days, your customers are paying you 15 days late.
4) Multiply one day's credit sales times the days late pay. This equals the cash that should be in your bank account.
5) Take that cash times your interest rate. That is the pure interest cost of slow pay. (Doesn't include billing costs, collection costs, etc.)

Do I have your attention now? So, to fix this problem will take diligence!

Chapter 13

CREDIT POLICY MANUAL

A business requirement

Does your company have a written credit policy? Many of my clients, even those that extend six-figure credit lines, don't have credit policy manuals, which can be a huge mistake usually punctuated with big bad debt write-offs or even from friends of the owner. If your company has been operating without such a manual, it's time to formalize your credit process. Here's why:

1. A manual will protect your company. When your credit manager is the only person who knows how credit decisions are made, he or she becomes indispensable. If he or she is ill or no longer on the job because of death, retirement, or termination, the company is at substantial risk when credit decisions must be made. When you don't have a manual and your credit manager has left, it can take replacements forever to get up to speed.

2. When you write a policy manual, it forces you to think about and clarify your credit procedures. Going through the policy-writing process will help you learn your credit policies and make them better. You can spot problems and correct them. When your policies are put in writing, you will have a well-thought-out systematic procedure to follow and not have to rely on your credit people's instincts.

3. A written credit policy also will provide clarity and consistency in your company's communications internally and externally. Internally, different people will not be giving your sales and other personnel different information. Externally, your customers will be treated consistently and they can easily be told exactly what they need to submit on their financial statement to be granted certain lines of credit. This will make your company more professional and business like.

Internally, the greatest benefit of a written manual may be to eliminate the petty animosity that typically exists between credit and sales departments. If a written policy exists, your sales staff can clearly read and understand how and why credit decisions are made. This allows them to prioritize their prospects according to their credit-worthiness and focus their valuable prospecting time exclusively on viable accounts. They won't blame the credit people when their customers' applications are rejected.

If you're convinced that you need a written manual, the next step is to get it written, which can be easier said than done, especially since you probably have numerous pressing problems to solve every day. Start by pulling together a team with members who are knowledgeable about customer and credit issues. Don't just hand this project off to your credit manager without giving him or her guidance and input from other departments.

Before assembling the team, it's also a good idea to gather background information on your bad debts and slow-paying accounts. Try to detect similarities (particularly in classes of trade) in your problem and delinquent accounts. An excellent way to keep track of them is by using SIC (Standard Industrial Classification) numbers in the customer screen. Check with your General Ledger (GL) vendor about how to use and sort customers by their SIC codes.

The manual team

Select a team to draft your credit policy manual. Ideally, it should consist of the following members:

- The business owner(s)
- The credit manager (and staff)
- Sales department representative(s)
- Customer service department representative(s)

The key factor is to get input from representatives of all the facets of your company that may be involved in the credit process. Representatives from various areas could inform you about special needs or give you insights that you might not have otherwise known.

The writing process

To write a credit manual, here's how to proceed:

Step One

Create a flowchart of your existing credit system. Then identify what is working smoothly as well as the snags and problems. Find the answers to questions such as: a) when credit is initially checked, b) how and when credit limits are established, c) the effectiveness of the current credit hold situation, and d) ongoing credit maintenance. Examine all credit problems for trends, insights, and common factors. Don't be discouraged if your system isn't working well. You'll get the chance to improve it in step two.

Step Two

Draw a flowchart of your ideal credit system. If, under your existing system, new applicants' credit is not checked until the last minute, think about initiating pre-sales credit checks.

> **WARNING:** It's legal to run pre-sale credit checks on corporate entities, but not on individuals. When you've designed your ideal credit system and before you put it into action, check with your attorney to be sure your process complies with all national, state and local laws in all respects.

Although credit policies will differ from company to company and vary according to customer trends, consider the following:

Setting **credit dollar ranges** for amounts such as:

- Less than $1,000.
- $1,000 to $9,999.
- $10,000 to $24,999.
- $25,000 to $50,000.
- Greater than $50,000.

For each range, specify precisely what information you will require applicants to submit in order for you to evaluate their applications and monitor whatever credit you extend. For instance, you may wish to require them to produce three years of financial statements on credit requests for more than $25,000 depending on your risk tolerance.

Creating specific requirements or limitations for certain industry or classes-of-trade specific. If your company has had difficulty getting timely payments from a certain industry, for example in petroleum, single owner truckers can be difficult, you may decide to require personal guarantees from them.

Writing user-friendly, but comprehensive credit applications and efficient application processing procedures. The idea here is to make it easy for applicants to complete and submit all essential information so that you don't waste time and effort chasing down any of it. Also, the forms must provide all information necessary for you to make sound credit decisions. At Meridian Associates, we have sample credit applications and have participants at our live events exchange their credit applications. It's amazing to see the variety of applications and critical items many businesses overlook.

Establishing credit limit guidelines that specify the financial criteria that your customers must meet to qualify for various credit amounts. These guidelines will be largely dictated by your credit staff's knowledge and experience. Although credit personnel often have difficulty clearly expressing how they make credit decisions, it's imperative that you nail down their thought processes in concrete, standardized, non-subjective guidelines that will form the basis of your credit policies.

Drafting collection procedures. Again, you may want different procedures for different dollar amounts of credit or different classes of trade. Each of these levels should be spelled out in your manual.

Monitoring accounts. When you create credit-monitoring procedures, allow for different monitoring frequencies, depths of information and analysis that are based on dollar amounts, established limits, and types of account.

Final review. When the team has met and decided on the details of your credit policy, you may wish to hand off various functions for expedience. For instance, assigning the typing to a clerical staff member or financial verifications to a member of your accounting department. Once typed, the entire team should review and edit the manual for accuracy, clarity, to incorporate last minute developments, and to give their final blessing.

Ideally, the team approach will help make your credit manual clear so it can be easily read and followed by all of your staff and applicants. Using a team, should also help insure that your manual includes all the requirements and policies that your company wants to adopt.

Action items

- Assemble a team to write your credit policy manual.
- Set a firm date for the manual to be written.
- Have your attorney review the draft of your credit policy manual.
- Record the actions taken in the Success Tracker below
- When estimating cash, think personnel time as well as receivables and bad debt.

Credit Policy Success Tracker

Measurable Goal	
Reward(s)	
Consequence(s)	

Action	Start Date	Target Finish	Cash Estimate	Person Responsible

Chapter 14

RISK RATING ACCOUNTS RECEIVABLE

Results in fewer bad debts

Do you always rate risks before you extend credit? If not, you should. Recently a company called me that had lost over $400,000 on one account. They wish they had been using a risk rating!

Risk rating is essential because it helps you avoid bad debts (big or small) and it streamlines and standardizes your credit processes. It also provides precise criteria that your personnel can consistently follow.

Rating risks makes your credit process more efficient. It allows your people to spend less time and effort on low-risk accounts and frees them up to examine high-risk accounts more closely.

If you routinely extend credit, creating and following a risk-rating system is essential. Here are guidelines for establishing an effective system.

Simplicity. To be effective, your system must be easy to understand and use. A five-point system based upon the risk of non-payment usually works best. The five categories are:

> 1 = Minimal perceived nonpayment risk.
> 2 = Less than average nonpayment risk.
> 3 = Average nonpayment risk.
> 4 = Above average nonpayment risk.
> 5 = High nonpayment risk.

Risk-rating systems with more than five categories are cumbersome and not as effective as a five-category system. Even the largest lenders, those that give the most complex loans, use only five rating categories. Those with fewer categories may not be as effective.

Credit matrix. Make sure that your rating system provides clear, written definitions of how all of your risk ratings will be determined. Use a rating formula made up of a combination of (a) your sales profit margin, (b) the expected credit limit, (c) the customer's industry, (d) the customer's ability and (e) the customer's willingness to pay. Let's call these items your credit matrix and look at each of them in greater detail.

(a). *Sales margin*. The lower your gross-profit margin, the higher your potential risk. If you make a gross profit of 75%- on a customer that doesn't pay its bill, it will only take you a one paying customer to recoup the loss and still come out ahead. However, if you only make 5% gross profit, you will need 19 more customers to purchase that same product to cover your loss. Use your typical margins to define your specific margin levels for each of the five risk ratings.

(b). *Amount of credit*. Assign dollar credit limits to each of the five risk-rating categories. The amounts you assign should be based on sound business reasons, and should not be arbitrary. For example, in the petroleum industry, it's typical that any credit limit below $5,000 might not be worth spending time on so they would automatically give them a "1" ranking. Similarly, this industry might classify a request for amounts over $100,000 as a "5." For smaller businesses, the limits might be less; say $1,000 and $25,000 respectively. The limits you set should reflect your company's capacity to absorb bad debts and the nature of the marketplace and your industry.

(c). *Industry*. In this evaluation, the main question is, "How risky is the customer's industry?" Do you serve industries that, because of concentration of receivables dollars or other unique circumstances, should be ranked as risky? Probably. Rate all of the industries you serve according to their risk and factor in that risk when you rate individual customers within those industries.

EXAMPLE: Most banks label all general contractors category 5 risks until the contractors establish multi-year track records that justify higher ratings. Risky industries for you might be lumber, mining, or those unique to your area.

(d) *Customer's Ability to Pay*. Let's use two risk-rating criteria to evaluate a customer's ability to pay because this factor is so crucial. The two criteria are:

> 1. The customer's short-term ability to pay as measured by its available cash. Stress to your credit personnel that they should always remember that cold, hard cash pays accounts, nothing else. The amount of available cash is calculated by combining:
>
>   a. The customer's cash with
>   b. The cash it can obtain through lines of credit.

EXAMPLE: An applicant with $25,000 in cash, a $1,000,000 credit line, and $950,000 drawn on the credit line, would have $75,000 in available cash. If it requests $100,000 in credit, it should be classified as a category 5 risk or possibly a COD account.

> 2. The customer's length of time in business. Some lenders use time in business as a separate matrix item, but we prefer to factor it into the customer's ability to pay.

The best indicator of long-term payment ability, especially when a customer is under duress, is its net worth (total assets minus total liabilities). If a customer is short on available cash, but has good equity in its assets, then the danger of bankruptcy is low.

Take the net worth calculation one step further to determine the equity percentage. This is done by dividing net worth by total assets. Banks use 25% equity as a benchmark, so you might place customers with 25% equity in category 3.

EXAMPLE: Customer with $1,050,000 in assets and net worth of $262,500. This is 25% equity ($262,500 divided by $1,050,000) and would be a "3" rated account. If the equity is anything under 20%, the customer should be in category 4. Anything 15% or less is a definite a 5, while 50% or more is a 1.

(e) *Willingness to pay.* Unfortunately, some customers have the ability to pay creditors, but not the willingness. The best way to check their willingness is by reviewing credit reports from companies such as D&B or Experian. These reports will give you the customer's credit history and tell you how promptly it is paying its current creditors.

TIP: Always require trade references on your credit applications and check on them. However, remember that most customers will not put down names of those they have not paid or paid slowly.

Checklists

Create a checklist for all accounts that involve credit decisions, and insist that your credit staff verifies that it examined all the credit criteria discussed in your credit matrix. Have them assign a risk rating for each criteria and an overall customer risk score. Accounts below a certain dollar limit may not require the full checklist, but those above the minimum level must have a completed matrix and overall score. The overall score should be posted and available directly on your computer files.

Action items

- Create a system for rating credit risks.
- Use your risk-rating system for all new credit requests.
- Review your existing accounts and rate their risks.
- Post the risk-rate score on your account files.
- Complete the Success Tracker below:

Risk Rating Cash Success Tracker

Measurable Goal	
Reward(s)	
Consequence(s)	

Action	Start Date	Target Finish	Cash Estimate	Person Responsible

Chapter 15

APPROPRIATE CUSTOMER CREDIT LIMITS

The combination of slow-pay and no-pay customers can destroy your company's cash flow. As a business owner, when money isn't coming in, you can lose sleep just from the fear that lack of cash can put you out of business. So reduce your cash drain by setting *appropriate* credit limits on all your customers, and do it now.
Yes, this means actually determining the right amount of credit that you will give each and every customer. And yes, it's a big order. However, if you figure your own sleep factor plus the potential savings it can bring your company, you *will* find the time and resources to complete this project.

Here's how to determine the amount of credit your customer can afford to pay:

Get needed information

Information is the most critical ingredient in making sound decisions. When you don't have the necessary facts, you're just guessing. Here's how to get the information you need to make the right credit decisions:

- *Credit Application.* It starts with a good customer credit application. Don't have a credit application? Then, you need one now. Thanks to the internet, samples for all industries are readily available Include a "credit amount requested" and "trade references section" on your application. To insure your application adheres to state and federal law, have your attorney review your document before rolling out.

- *Financial Statements*. Insist on getting a current financial statement from every applicant that wants more than $10,000 in trade credit. Clearly state that this is your policy right on your credit application.

- *Credit Bureau Report*. This report will tell you how much credit other vendors have extended to the applicant and the applicant's payment promptness history. Credit reports often contain valuable sales, profit, balance sheet, and management info as well. Certain credit reporting agencies may

57

give you a group discount because of your affiliation with trade or industry associations. Check with them.

- *Customer Sales Estimate*. For new customers, have your salespeople estimate how much they expect the customer to purchase each month. When you review their estimates, remember that salespeople tend to be a bit optimistic.

Analyze information

Decide if the amount of credit the customer requested is reasonable in light of your salesperson's monthly customer-purchasing estimate. Determine whether the amount of business you hope to get from the customer will justify your granting the amount of credit that the customer wants. If the amount of credit requested substantially exceeds the customer's anticipated purchases, discuss the difference with the salesperson. If the requested credit amount is less than the salesperson's estimate, try to initially qualify the customer for the amount it seeks.

Check all major trade references. Contact those that the customer listed as references in the application, which of course will usually be good references. Also check the credit bureau report. Specifically find out where the customer currently buys its main supplies. Then determine the amount of its credit line and how it pays.

Analyze the customer's available cash position. Remember that cash, not promises, pays your invoice. First, find out from the customer's bank how much cash is in the customer's accounts and investments. Ideally, the amount of credit you extend should not be more than the customer's average cash balance, unless it has a working capital line of credit with additional cash available to borrow.

EXAMPLE: Potential customer requests credit of $10,000. Check the ledger cash balance on its financial statements. That balance should be $10,000 or more. If less, then make sure that potential customer has no less than $10,000 in borrowing availability on its bank credit line. If no $10,000 between the two, no account with you.

TIP: On all accounts, check the credit bureau balance sheet for trends in the customer's payment history. Look out for a declining cash position, particularly when it's coupled with increasing trade payables. These two together should raise a big red flag that the customer is experiencing a cash crunch. Also keep in mind that the customer might be coming to you because it can't pay their bill with other suppliers. If you detect either of these trends, make the customer a COD account because it could be a bad debt waiting to happen.

Finally, look at the net worth on the customer's balance. Never extend a company more credit than its owners have invested.

Establish credit limits

Now, you're ready to set a dollar figure on the customer's credit limit. The maximum credit you extend should never be more than:

- The maximum amount the customer expects to use.
- The cash that the customer readily has available for payment.
- The customer's net worth.

Let's test your credit skills in the following credit request examples:

EXAMPLE #1 Smith Construction requested a $15,000 line of credit on its application. Your salesperson indicates that Smith will buy $20,000 in a billing cycle.

Smith submitted financial statements that show it had $10,345 cash through last year-end and that it has $12,005 cash now. Its bank reports that it has carried an average cash balance of $10,530 this year.

Smith also has a bank line of $225,000, on which it owed $152,000 at last year-end and $147,500 now. The company's net worth is currently $334,000, and profit for the year is $75,000. Last year Smith suffered a loss of $51,000. All financial trends and ratios appear to be improving.

The credit report shows mostly prompt payment with one chronically delinquent account in the high four figure-range. All trade references provided indicate prompt payment.

> *Appropriate Credit Limit*: **$15,000**
>
> In arriving at this figure, I ignored the salesperson's optimistic estimate and approved the amount of credit that the customer requested. Although Smith's cash balance is less than the amount of its credit-line request, it has enough funds available on its line of credit to make our payment.

EXAMPLE #2 Now, let's says that everything for Smith Construction is the same except they have no credit line.

> *Appropriate Credit Limit*: **$10,000**
>
> The credit granted must be lower without access to the credit line. The credit decision now turns of the amount of cash is available to the customer, which is estimated best by the customer's average checking account balances for this year.

EXAMPLE #3 Let's reverse the financial statements and say that last year the customer made a $75,000 profit, but this it has incurred a loss. Reverse the balance sheet information as well.

> *Appropriate Credit Limit*: **Nothing**
>
> Credit should not be extended until the reason for the customer's loss is determined and an informed credit decision can be made.

Action items

- List the four ways to obtain financial information on a credit applicant.
- Analyze the financial data and check credit references.
- Set credit limits for each applicant.
- Complete the Success Tracker below:

Customer Credit Limit Cash Success Tracker

Measurable Goal	
Reward(s)	
Consequence(s)	

Action	Start Date	Target Finish	Cash Estimate	Person Responsible

Bonus Chapter 16

SUPER SPEEDY COLLECTIONS VIA 100% EFT

Get every one of your customers on EFT (Electronic Funds Transfer). If this sounds like a pipe dream, it's not. Some of my clients at Meridian have converted *all* of their existing customers to EFT, and most of my clients now insist on mandatory EFT terms for all their new customers. Using EFT has dramatically increased their cash flow, and some report that they are receiving customer payments BEFORE their due dates. Now they are sleeping like babies!

Converting to EFT is not as difficult as you may think. It's well worth the efforts when you consider the savings you'll receive. All you have to do is follow these ten simple steps:

1. *Contact your software vendor.* General ledger (GL) software vendors have programs that make EFT easy and user-friendly for your staff. Your vendor will help you understand the EFT process as it relates to your receivables accounting and collections process. Plus, they can refer you to other businesses that use the same GL process. If you use "off-the-shelf" popular software, it's even easier.

2. *Contact references.* Before you commit to an EFT system, ask your GL vendor for names of its EFT customers and then call a few that are in businesses most like yours. Talk directly to their EFT people. Question them about the software, its advantages, disadvantages, quirks, and tricks. If the vendor will be providing services, ask about them. No one will give you better and more relevant information than those who are on the same GL system. In addition, they may tell you about great shortcuts and efficiency enhancers that you can adopt, plus be upfront about their problems with the vendor and/or system.

3. *Contact your bank.* By now, banks are well versed on EFT transactions and are highly experienced in helping companies implement them. In the event you do business with a very small or technically unsophisticated bank that can't help you with EFT processes, and assuming they are not willing to implement the process, switch banks. EFT is too important to your cash flow to delay. You need a savvy, up-to-date bank to grow and move forward.

4. *Educate your staff.* You can set up a terrific, state-of-the-art accounting system that works wonderfully, but if your sales and customer service staff doesn't buy into it, they won't sell it effectively. As soon as you begin to explore EFT, bring your sales and customer service staff into the process. Show them why EFT will be good for them and good for customers to get them to buy-in. Make them feel that they have a stake in moving to EFT.

5. *Work out the bugs.* Implementing any new system takes time and presents problems. So face your first problems, and make your first mistakes, where it will do the least harm. Practice on a sister company or a tolerant, loyal customer. Beta test your new system on them and work out any unforeseen problems before you roll the EFT system out to all of your customers.

6. *Attorney review.* Have all EFT documents reviewed by your attorney, particularly if your EFT agreement will become a part of your new customer application. Have your attorney explain each and every provision to you so that you in turn can make them clear to your staff and your customers. If you change or paraphrase any language, be sure it stays within the law. Better yet, run _all_ changes you make by your legal counsel.

7. *Create a marketing plan.* To convert your existing customers to EFT, you may have to give them inducements and train your sales force in new areas.

EXAMPLE: Successful marketers have facilitated EFT switches by offering their customers attractive terms that save everyone money even after discounts are factored into the equation. A client I work with found that it could offer its customers as much as a 3% discount for net 10 terms and 2% for net 20 terms and still be ahead cash wise. Prior to EFT, its customers were stretching its non-discounted 30-day terms to about 60 days. The owner loves the new cash flow and the team likes the easier process.

8. *Set conversion goals.* The first EFT conversions most petroleum companies make are with their gasoline dealer accounts. Then, they follow with other high volume customers. Who are your largest dollar accounts? Have your accounting and sales staff set realistic timetables and a series of achievable weekly conversion goals. Your ultimate goal should be to convert of all of your accounts.

In rural areas, it's not uncommon for long-term agricultural accounts to be EFT resistant. However, attractive terms usually will overcome this resistance. Old-timers may not want to jump on the EFT bandwagon, and it may take extra effort by your sales staff to convert them.

TIP: By just changing the name of their EFT program to the new name EZ Pay, one of my clients more than tripled its conversion rate! Come up with a user-friendly name for your EFT program!

9. *Monitoring and feedback.* When your system is ready, its process is clear, training has been completed, goals set, and marketing commenced, hold regular meetings to review conversion rates and compare them with your goals. Also get feedback from your staff on any problems or resistance they encountered.

At meetings, problems and solutions should be openly discussed. If you can't come up with solutions, other non-competing companies can help. Companies that collect more than 50% of their accounts via EFT have probably encountered and conquered the problems you face. So understand that they are not insurmountable, and ask for help.

10. *Celebrate success.* As you meet your monthly goals, celebrate. EFT success creates positive cash flow and saves your company money. Quantify those savings so you know exactly how much you've saved. Then, show your appreciation, and consider expressing your gratitude by sharing the wealth with the staff that spearheaded the conversion.

Celebrations don't have to be lavish. Often, a pizza lunch and public recognition of the team are all that's needed to keep your EFT team pumped up and working toward reaching your 100% conversion goal. Of course you could give nice fat bonuses to the team when they meet the 100% target because few things say thank you better than cash. Either way, celebrate success, show your appreciation, and make it fun.

Action items

- Decide to convert all of your accounts to EFTs.
- Contact your General Ledger vendor for programs consistent with your system.
- Speak with companies with your systems about their experience after converting to EFT.
- Record your company's actions implementing EFT in the Success Tracker:

EFT Conversion Cash Success Tracker

Measurable Goal	
Reward(s)	
Consequence(s)	

Action	Start Date	Target Finish	Cash Estimate	Person Responsible

Bonus Chapter 17

SEVEN STEP PLAN TO FEWER BAD DEBTS

Bad debts poison business. Customers who can't or won't pay their bills kill their suppliers' cash flow and their profits. Unless you reduce your arrearages, you may find yourself constantly struggling to stay afloat.

What can you do about it? Plenty! Start by using these seven proven steps. Some of them I've discussed before, but they're so critical that they bear repeating. The seven steps are:

1. *Create written Credit Policy.* If you don't have a written credit policy manual, go back to Bonus Chapter 12 and write one now. When your manual is written, your company's policy will no longer be ambiguous; it will be clear and easy for everyone to understand. Hold your credit manager accountable to periodically review and modify your credit policy; it should be examined at least once each year.

2. *Require complete applications.* When we ask our clients to analyze their bad-debt accounts, it's amazing how many were granted credit even though they submitted incomplete applications. Insist on getting complete information before you even think about extending credit—to any applicant. Make missing information on an application a red flag for your sales and credit personnel that cause the complete credit process to stop.

Explicitly state your requirement that credit applications must be fully completed in your credit policy. Clearly explain that incomplete applications will not be processed, and say how they will be handled. Choose the policy that's best for you and be consistent. Some companies return incomplete applications to their sales people. While others have their credit personnel have the prospective customer provide the missing information and don't get their sales force involved.

3. ***Set Credit Department Goals.*** Every company should set clear credit goals and regularly monitor them. Those goals can include:
- A certain percentage on current accounts,
- Earning specified amounts of stated dollars,
- Target Days Sales Outstanding (DSO)
- Decreasing or eliminating write-offs, etc.

> **Caution:** Sometimes when a company has a DSO goal, a clever credit clerk will "write-off" an old account (which means delete it from receivables) to hit their target which causes a bad debt expense. So don't have DSO goal without concurrent bad debt write-off goal.

Less common, but equally effective goals include accepting only completed credit applications, annually reviewing a target percent of customer-credit files, and risk-rating all credit applications. No matter what goals you choose to set, the process of setting them will make you more aware of the importance of being paid on time.

4. ***Use a risk rating matrix.*** See Chapter 13 for a more detailed discussion of risk rating systems.

5. ***Establish a monitoring system.*** Credit doesn't begin and end with the first sale; it can continue for years. Many accounts start well; the customers pay promptly and fully, but then change. For years their payments can come in promptly, like clockwork, but suddenly they pay slowly or not at all.

Monitor all your accounts regularly and note any trends. Give closer, more frequent attention to accounts with high-risk ratings and those that are for large amounts of credit. At the least, high dollar, high-risk accounts should be reviewed quarterly. Put accountability systems in place for both departments and individuals to be sure that reviews are standardized and take place on a timely basis.

6. ***Require call frequency.*** Instruct your sales professionals to frequently visit large dollar and high-risk accounts. While on site, have them speak with their customers' employees in order to get a sense of the company's pulse. Also, tell them to solicit feedback from drivers who serve these customers

because drivers often have good intuition and hear rumblings about accounts that may be having financial woes.

7. Conduct weekly cross-departmental meetings. Members of your sales and credit departments should participate together in weekly meetings. At first, the combination may be like oil and water, but with time and coaching, they'll unify and become a team. After all, it's to everyone's benefit to have sales and credit talking and working cooperatively on both new and existing accounts. Also, consider inviting your drivers to rotate in and out of the credit meetings. They can often provide terrific first-hand information about accounts that your sales and credit personnel might otherwise miss.

TIP: Tighten your policies and procedures. When you create a written credit policy, require complete applications, set credit goals, rate risks, monitor effectively, call frequently on accounts, and hold weekly interdepartmental meetings, you can make getting paid the normal course of business it should be.

Action items

- Review the seven steps to fewer bad debts.
- Require all credit applications to be fully completed.
- Establish a procedure to handle incomplete credit applications.
- Fill in the actions taken in the *7 Quick Fixes* Success Tracker below:

Bad Debt Reduction Cash Success Tracker

Measurable Goal	
Reward(s)	
Consequence(s)	

Action	Start Date	Target Finish	Cash Estimate	Person Responsible

Bonus Section II

INVENTORY POWER

You've come to this bonus section because you realize you have serious amounts of cash tied up in inventory. That's your cash sunk in idle stock not making you a dime. And, you not only have the cash out of pocket, you also get to count it, take care of it, protect it, clean it and reconcile it too! So, I'm going to assume you've come to this section to get serious, to take a powerful hold on your inventory practices. This is where you will need to dig in. It will take far more work than the quick fixes.

To see if it's worth the work, you need to understand the magnitude of your lost profit from your existing inventory management practices. There is a calculator in the Quick Fix Toolbox, but you can also do this manually using the following steps:

Excess Inventory Calculator

1) Determine your <u>Actual</u> days supply of inventory you normally keep on hand by doing the following calculation:
    a. Using your latest financial statement, determine one day's cost of goods sold. (For example, if you are looking at a P&L for one month, divide the full month's Cost of Goods Sold by 30 days. If looking at a one-year statement, divided COGS by 365 days.)
    b. Divide your total inventory dollars on your most recent balance sheet by one day's COGS from step (a) The result is your <u>Actual</u> days inventory supply on hand.
2) Calculate your <u>Ideal</u> inventory (1.5 times supplier frequency – see Quick Fix #3 for details.)
3) Subtract ideal number of days from Step 2 from Actual Days (step 1). This equals your <u>Excess</u> inventory days.
4) Multiply Excess Days (Step 3) by one day's Cost of Goods Sold times your bank line interest and then add warehousing, counting, cleaning and other costs. This is the total cost, the actual lost profit from weak inventory systems.

Is this number large enough for me to have your total attention now? Do you desperately need that cash or could you use it to grow your company? If so, to fix this costly problem will take diligence! Will it be worth it?

That depends on the magnitude of your lost profits you just calculated. Only you can determine if it's worth it to you to expend the time and energy it will take to create more powerful, effective inventory systems in your business.

If you are committed, let's get started!

Bonus Chapter 18

REDUCE INVENTORY FOR HIGHER PROFITS

Inventory is expensive. Every $100,000 in inventory you stock costs your company approximately $10,000 each year just to maintain.

When business managers, CFOs, and owners add up how much inventory they have on hand, they frequently find that it exceeds my recommendation of no more than 1.5 times each supplier delivery. As a result, they find that they have more money invested in stock than they should.

EXAMPLE: According to my formula, a store that sells $2,175 worth of inside goods per day (no fuel in my industry), or about $65,000 per month, should have no more than $23,925 invested in its inventory. If its inventory is even more, say $38,000, the store has over $14,000 more in stock than it needs.

You've already done your savings estimate at the beginning of this section. If you skipped over that calculation, make a quick estimate of how much a 20% reduction in your payables and inventory processes will save you. You could be surprised how much it can affect your bottom line.

So, how is it possible to reduce inventory without losing customers? Try these two strategies:

1) Identify slow or non-moving products. Take a good look at stock reports to learn exactly what items are moving and how quickly they move.

2) Then, when you know exactly what the slow or non-moving items are, find out why they're not flying out the door. Products typically move slowly because of three factors:

    a. Lack of customer demand.
    b. Poor merchandising.
    c. Overpricing.

Let's look at each of these factors more closely, and how they can be addressed.

Lack of customer demand

TIP: If your customers do not buy a product, try to get the vendor that supplied it to take it back. Whenever a vendor asks you to take on a new product, insist that the vendor agrees in the contract that you can return any unsold items. Make sure that you can return the items to the vendor for cash or credit and not just to the manufacturer.

If you have slow-moving goods that are not covered by a buy-back agreement, and the vendor refuses to take them back, unload them in a quick sale. Price them for a fast turn over, and consider any cash you get to be a bonus.

WARNING: Make sure not to mistakenly reorder slow moving products that finally sell.

Poor merchandising

If customer demand is still pretty good for a slow-moving product, you may have a merchandising problem. Make sure that your customers can easily find the product. If they can't, move it to a better, more visible location or place it near companion or complementary products.

Overpricing

The only way to learn if pricing is your problem is to comparison-shop the product. Keep in mind that the overall character of your store could impact your ability to price. For example, if your store or location attracts price-sensitive shoppers, most of your shoppers won't buy higher-priced goods. To move the product, you may have to sell it at a lower price than your competitors. On the other hand, if your location caters to higher-end, less price-sensitive shoppers, you can charge more for the product than your competitors and it will still sell.

Secret Weapon -- Reduce SKUs

Businesses that reduce the number of SKUs (stock keeping units) by 20% gain a significant increase in profits. SKUs are unique codes that identify a product by its brand, model, version, and size. The small-size box of a particular brand of detergent has its own unique SKU number while the large-size box of that brand has a different SKU number.

TIP: Take a hard look at how many different sizes you stock of the products you carry. Do you really need to carry chips in the small bag, the 99-cent grabber, the regular size, and the super family size? Analyze your sales by package sizes to discover which of those sizes you can discontinue without making much of a dent in your total sales.

If you have a scanning system, the task should be easy. If you don't scan, here's how to identify package sizes you could eliminate.

- Ask your clerks and location managers to identify products that are not moving or that move slowly. Find out which package sizes they think could be dropped.
- Check your vendor's purchasing records to learn which products have been selling most briskly and which have been lagging.

WARNING: Some of your vendors may have objectives that conflict with yours. They may have sales targets that may not be consistent with your customers' demands. For example, if you're thinking about eliminating two package sizes of chips, your vendor may pressure you to continue stocking them if it receives premiums for selling those sizes. So, make your decisions based upon your customers' buying habits, not because of vendor pressure.

Discontinuing certain SKUs can be tricky. You can stock a size that sells well, but can be replaced by a larger or smaller size with no loss of sales. On the other hand, if you stopped selling a size, your customers might not buy the sizes you still carried. Often, it takes some experimenting to get it right.

When you reduce your SKUs by 20%, your overhead costs will also decrease. Essentially, you will be eliminating 20% of your staff's workload in areas including payables, order verification, inventory controls, and more. So, in addition to creating better turn over for your remaining products and gaining higher gross profits, you'll get a double whammy by also saving on your operating costs.

> **TIP:** Reducing your SKUs is like pruning your garden. When you eliminate dead wood and weaker growth, it leaves more room and light for the stronger items to grow. They can get more of the attention and nourishment you provide, which will make them more likely to thrive.

Action items

- Identify your slow or non-moving products.
- Find out the reasons why those items are moving slowly or not at all.
- Identify 20% of your SKUs that you could stop stocking.
- Fill in the Success Tracker below:

Inventory Reduction Cash Success Tracker

Measurable Goal	
Reward(s)	
Consequence(s)	

Action	Start Date	Target Finish	Cash Estimate	Person Responsible

Bonus Chapter 19

INVENTORY
DO YOU HAVE IT RIGHT YET?

Prior to one of Meridian's live seminar events, we offered one of our loyal clients, a company that operated convenience stores and quick serve restaurants (typical big name franchises), a free inventory analysis on the condition that we could present our findings at the event. The client eagerly agreed.

We asked our client to select the site she wanted analyzed. She chose a location that performed well a few years back, but recently experienced a steady decline despite our client's extensive efforts. Management had invested lots of money to give this combined convenience store and quick serve restaurant facility a major face lift and to upgrade its food offerings, but despite all the spiffying up, the unit's sales continued to slump.

Our first step in the analysis was to have a demographic study conducted. The study showed that management had based its food offerings on mistaken assumptions about its customers' buying preferences. As the centerpiece of its remodel, our client had embarked on a co-branded hamburger offering. But do you know what our demographic study revealed? Hamburgers were the wrong choice! The bulk of the restaurant's customers weren't hamburger eaters — they were hot dog lovers.

This simple error, this wrong assumption, was costly, astoundingly costly. When we showed our client our data, the CFO quickly realized in retrospect that the restaurant's sales began to slip soon after it began to push hamburgers.

What customers want

Not all inventory choices are as simple as deciding whether to sell hamburgers or hotdogs, but a key to retail success is offering your customers what they want to buy. Determining what those items might be can seem like a daunting task, until you conduct a low-cost, demographics study. (If you are a wholesaler, keep reading! While I've used a retail example, the concepts apply to you as well.)

Thanks to computer wizardry, demographic information can now be extracted from virtually whatever area or series of areas you want. They no longer have to be confined to zip codes. Now you can learn how many people live in a specific area or areas, and get breakdowns according to their ages, family sizes, education, income, buying patterns, and lots of other information.

EXAMPLE: If your business is on a major highway that runs north to south, you can obtain demographic profiles of all the households on a 10-mile stretch of that highway using a one-mile parameter on each side of the highway. If you want figures from two unconnected circular areas or a circular area plus a rectangular strip — no problem. Using state of the art technology, a good demographics firm will get information on whatever areas you select for your study and the proof you need.

Demographics studies can tell you exactly what your customers have been buying. Although they won't inform you about hot new products, they will provide you with information on the staples your customers buy.

Cost effectiveness

Doesn't it make sense to buy and stock what your customers will buy? Think how much you can save by reducing returns and slow moving stock. Don't shy away from demographic studies because you're afraid that they will be too expensive; they're an investment you should make. Demographic studies are extremely cost-effective; the information you can get from a study of one site for one month will probably exceed the study's cost and help you boost your revenues.

Companies that obtain demographic information and then specifically design their offerings at each of their sites to meet their customers' preferences, have a huge edge over national and regional cookie-cutter operations. Think about it. You simply can't stock a store in my hometown of Weatherford, Texas with the same exact products as your locations in Tampa, Florida or Bangor, Maine and expect to maximize sales in all three locations. At least one, if not all, will suffer. In a single town, you may find major differences in your customers' buying preferences at different locations. Each of your individual stores must accommodate its particular customers if you hope to obtain above-average sales and profits at each location.

TIP: Monitor your sales to see if you're offering the right products. If you find that you are, your challenge will be to stock the right amount of the products your customers want. If you find that you're not providing what your customers want, eliminate what isn't selling and bring in what will.

Stocking formula

Another critical question is how much inventory should you stock? If you've read your Quick Fixes, you already know the formula -- only stock 1.5 times the amount of your supplier's delivery frequency. If your supplier delivers a dozen cases of cleaning fluid to you once a week, your maximum inventory should never exceed 1.5 times 7 days (weekly delivery) or 18 cases per week. If you purchase at this rate, you will receive 10-11 days of inventory per shipment or about 36 – 38 turns per year. If your supplier delivers twice per week, your stocking rate should be no more than 6 days of product or 60 turns. By the way, this formula works for non-retail goods as well.

Action items

- Order a demographic study for each site you operate.
- Use the study results to modify your offerings so you only carry what your customers will regularly buy.
- Stock no more than 1.5 times the amount of your supplier's regular deliveries.
- Fill in the Success Tracker below:

Get Inventory Right Cash Success Tracker

Measurable Goal	
Reward(s)	
Consequence(s)	

Action	Start Date	Target Finish	Cash Estimate	Person Responsible

Bonus Chapter 20

AUTOMATED INVENTORY CONTROL

How much time and money does your company waste because you're not taking advantage of automated inventory control? In most cases, the answer is plenty — whether you're a wholesaler or retailer.
The good news is that recent enhancements to software mean that your company can quickly spend less time and money managing its inventory. However, you must have the courage to use this software capability.

Software can't select the right products for you to carry, but it can help a lot. It also cannot decide on the best ways for you to promote products; that's your call. What it can do is:

- Accurately report, and frequently forecast, customer trends and demands.
- Alert you to old or non-moving products.
- Expedite your order and replenishment process.

Getting started

To begin automating your inventory controls, start simply. Then move into more sophisticated areas.

Use your system to alert you about slow-moving products. Your system probably already has this ability, but check with your vendor. Your vendor probably knows of additional applications or twists that would be ideal for your business or your products.

Here's how the alert function works. For each product, enter how many units you want to stock; that number will be your target supply. The computer will then compare the number of units in your inventory with your target supply, and will send you an exception report when you exceed your target supply. As I've suggested, for efficiency and cost savings, set your target supply at 1.5 times the supplier delivery frequency.

As new inventory is delivered and the sales cycle progresses, your system will check the total supply of each product against the target. Daily reports will be printed and stocks of products that exceed their targets will be identified.

EXAMPLE: If your target inventory for floor polish is 11 days, and after today's delivery, you have a 15-days' supply, the system would automatically print a report to alert you that your supply exceeds your target. It would itemize your target amount, the amount on hand, and the overage or shortage for each item.

Exception reports are critical to good inventory management. In fact, in more sophisticated systems, projected targets (both higher and lower than the original targets) take into account seasonal or cyclical variations. Systems can also project targets based upon last year's sales and your company's rate of growth. For the maximum effectiveness, exception reports should be issued for individual sites or locations, not company-wide.

Predicting demand

When your target inventory levels have been set and you're receiving exception reports, use your data to predict customer demand. In most businesses, inventory build-ups or shortages are due to changes in customers' buying habits.

> **TIP:** Analyze your exception reports to spot fluctuations in customer's buying patterns. Then figure out why those buying fluctuations occurred, and alter your company's purchases accordingly. Technology can't tell you if you're buying the right products, but it will sure let you know when you've chosen wrong.

Ordering

Next, use your system to order goods. If, at this stage, you are not yet linked on-line with your supplier, you will have to place your own orders. Create order triggers that are based upon your:

- Minimum inventory targets.
- Product turn-over rate.
- Supplier's lead-time.

Your system will generate orders based on your anticipated inventory level on the day when your supplier regularly delivers. Your system will factor in all of these considerations and then generate a report that tells you precisely how may units of each product you should order.

Linking

The final step is linking your system to your supplier's system so that it can generate orders and send them directly to your supplier without human intervention. After your supplier has received your order, you will receive a report informing you exactly what has been ordered and the supplier's confirmation.

WARNING: DO NOT enter into the automated ordering process until you test your minimum and maximum inventory targets for at least a few months. The last thing you want is to run out of product, so fine tune your system to make sure that every step works perfectly before you fully rely on it.

Automate first with a small supplier that furnishes you with just a few products rather than starting right off with your largest supplier. The less complicated the initial ordering process, the better. As you work the kinks out of the system and develop confidence in the systems you create, the more suppliers and products you can add.

If you rely on only one major supplier and it can accommodate automated ordering, ease your way into the process by starting with only a few selected products. Then add more products as you become comfortable with and confident in the system.

Throughout the process, move slowly. Start with one supplier and don't begin automating with others until your system with the first is running smoothly. Then automate your ordering process with other suppliers, but only add one at a time. Make sure that each system is operating flawlessly before you move on.

> **TIP:** Regularly keep in touch with all of your suppliers so that you always know if their products are available and can inform your customers that the items they want may have to be backordered.

Finally, once your system is running smoothly, don't become complacent. Continue to spend time anticipating your customers' needs, adding products, and marketing. Remember that automated inventory management is not a substitute for product development and marketing. However, it will free-up valuable time so you can focus on other areas more effectively. My favorite phrase is "turn data entry into data analysis." The more you automate, the more time you have to concentrate strategically on what new actions will drive your revenues and profits.

WARNING: *Learn from a Painful Experience*

A client had his tech guy develop what he thought was a foolproof system. A full 90 days post implementation, big problems were happening daily and he was baffled. Out of stocks, over stocks, the whole inventory was worse than before the automation. Digging into it, what he discovered shocked him. Because his Office Manager did not "trust" the automation, she had basically sabotaged the whole system by overriding the new automation so she could still input everything manually. What a mess! The moral to the story is automation must have total team buy-in to work.

Action items

- Use your automated system to alert you about slow moving products.
- Study the data produced by your system to predict customer demand.
- Link your system to your supplier to order goods.
- Get total team buy-in to automation.
- Fill in the Success Tracker below:

Inventory Automation Cash Success Tracker

Measurable Goal	
Reward(s)	
Consequence(s)	

Action	Start Date	Target Finish	Cash Estimate	Person Responsible

Bonus Chapter 21

TARGET MARKET AND REPLENISHMENT

In inventory management, nothing is more important than offering your customers the right product mix. Not only will your customers love you, but the right product mix will pay big dividends by reducing your costs and improving your cash flow. To give your customers the products they want, you must intimately and continually know who your customers are, and understand their needs, wants, and buying patterns.

Two distinct approaches can be used to gauge customer demand. The first, most common approach is to gather demographic data on customers within your geographic area, which I discussed in Ch. 16. The goal of these studies is to obtain the profile of your "typical customer" so you can match your product offerings to that profile. The idea is to minimize the guesswork and deliver what your customers will buy.

Target marketing

The other highly-successful approach is to identify a specific-customer group or target and then design product mixes that they will buy.

With target marketing, you don't have to start from scratch; it can work easily for businesses that are up and running. Existing operations can begin target marketing by profiling their best customers, and then fine-tuning their product line to meet those specific customers' needs. Conversely, the most profit-rich target market could be potential customers not yet buying from you. In that case, you would create a new product line to capture those customers.

EXAMPLE: If your target-customer group consists of professionals in households in which both spouses work, provide pickup and delivery service. Usually, you can charge a premium for this additional service.

When you decide which products to carry, turn your focus on marketing. Your marketing techniques, including your display-space strategies if retail, will determine what and how much inventory you should stock.

A number of exciting developments are now occurring in this area. Highly sophisticated computer models are beginning to emerge thanks to data warehousing where charge card or loyalty card transactions are captured by data analysis companies that can slice and dice all the aggregated data into meaningful reports. Literally millions of dollars of research are going into capturing customers' buying habits to more finely tune marketing strategies.

Replenishment

Now, you've reached the point where you know your target customer, what you want to buy and how much of it you should obtain, the next step is to establish procedures for replenishing your stock.

Ideally, your ordering system, including your replenishment process, has been automated and your vendors are linked on-line to your system. If so, the vendor is informed electronically when your stocks decrease a new supply will be ordered and delivered.

If you're still using a manual ordering system, invest some time to examine the efficiency (or inefficiency) of your replenishment and monitoring process.

> **TIP:** Focus particular attention on how you monitor information to spot shifts in customer demand, which is the Achilles Heel of most inventory systems. When you don't see and react to these shifts, your inventory can be loaded with slow or non-moving goods.

WARNING: Your big challenge is to create an inventory-monitoring system that will immediately detect acceleration and deceleration in your customers' purchasing patterns before your products become obsolete or your stocks deplete. However, even the best of these systems, require manpower.

Unfortunately, some companies may feel that they can't afford to put another person on their payroll, but frankly, you can't afford not to address inventory trends. If you get stuck with $50,000 worth of goods that you can't sell, you'll wish you had spent $35,000 on an employee to monitor inventory.

If you're wondering what such a system will do to "special buys," don't worry. Customer-demand trends will drive your purchasing so you won't be tempted to take on unnecessary inventory. In addition, you'll be able to negotiate deals on your fast-moving high volume products. Does this sound like you have a purchasing specialist? The answer is yes!

A professional purchasing specialist

To make your inventory-management processes most efficient and profitable, hire an astute purchasing specialist (PS). The person who becomes your PS may or may not be the same individual who monitors your customer-buying data. Whomever you choose, make sure that they have these two prerequisites:

1) Has experience on the vendor side. No one can negotiate with vendors better than someone has been a vendor.
2) Has superb negotiating skill. Even if your purchasing agent is an excellent negotiator, additional training can't hurt. Send him or her to seminars and workshops to add to, fine-tune, and polish his or her skills.

When you have effective systems in place, the answer to the question "What's not selling?" will always be, "Nothing."

Action items

- Identify a target group on which you could focus.
- Establish procedures for replenishing your inventory.
- Select a purchasing agent who has been a vendor and has strong negotiating skills.
- Fill in the Success Tracker on the next page:

Replenishment Cash Success Tracker

Measurable Goal	
Reward(s)	
Consequence(s)	

Action	Start Date	Target Finish	Cash Estimate	Person Responsible

Bonus Chapter 22

INVENTORY ERROR AND LOSS CHECKLIST

Inventory is vulnerable, even when you have it under lock and key. Inventory must be tightly controlled or you may end up with little or nothing to sell. We're constantly hearing upsetting stories about once successful businesses that were forced to shut down because of inventory losses or theft. Protect yourself. Take measures to safeguard your valuable inventory; the health of your business may depend on it. Review the list of typical inventory problems below, check those you should address, and consider implementing the practical solutions I recommend.

As you read this chapter, you'll see that I've previously addressed a few of these items. Please bear with me. The few points I've chosen to repeat are so essential that they can't be stressed often enough.

❏ *Overstocking*

<u>Solution</u>: Analyze your excess merchandise to determine why you're overstocked. Usually, it's because you're stocking the wrong products for your customer base or you ordered more of certain products than you sell. As I've suggested:

- o Return products to your vendors.
- o Sell items on the open market.
- o Consider moving goods to a location with a different customer base.
- o Order amounts consistent with your customers' demands.
- o Shoot for inventory levels of no more than 1.5 times vendor delivery frequency on any product.

❏ *Under stocking*

<u>Solution:</u> Reexamine your forecasts:

- o Update your forecasts so you can order enough items to meet the current demand.
- o If practical, get more frequent deliveries.
- o Review your sales-data history to anticipate trends in demand. If you have busy or slow seasons, determine why, and stock accordingly.
- o Regularly examine your goals and targets to assess the rate that you're building toward them. Then, increase your purchases to meet the anticipated demand.

❏ *Vendor errors*

<u>Solution</u>: Adopt a system that automatically gives you the price, category, amount of stock, and other vital information for the goods you receive. In an ideal world, your vendors would provide this data, and it and would flow right into your computer system so that the prices and other key information would always be correct. In reality; however, few vendors or marketers have the software sophistication to automatically and accurately provide you with the information you need.

- o Meet with your vendor and discuss installing a formalized information system.
- o Then, religiously get the data you receive into your system daily (manually if you must, automated better.)

❏ *Receiving errors*

<u>Solution:</u> Limit the number of people who are authorized to receive goods.

- o Train employees who receive goods diligently.

- Create standardized procedures for employees who receive goods to follow and require them to check or sign off on each step of each transaction.
- Make sure employees understand exactly what to do when delivered goods do not match the purchase order or when shortages or damage occur.
- Put procedures in place for lost invoices.
- If coding is a problem, find out the reasons and correct them.
- Create an employee accountability system.
- Reward your employees' accuracy.
- Do not tolerate employee errors.

❑ *Theft*

Solution: Face it, your employees, customers, vendors, subcontractors, and visitors can steal from you. Train your employees how to handle all of these types of theft. Yes, even train them about employee theft because the more they know about it, the less likely they will be to steal.

Technology can be a great deterrent to theft so install cameras prominently. Sophisticated camera systems can link video to register transactions allowing quick audit as needed.

❑ *Counting errors*

Solution: People will make mistakes; it's only human. And counting inventory can be tedious work that causes counters to wander, lose their concentration, and miscalculate.

The best solution is to give your counters training, to teach them how to concentrate, remain focused, and to be more accurate and thorough.

- Establish verification procedures for counting.
- Limit the number of people actually count inventory to be sure that they have all been thoroughly trained.

❏ *Cut-off errors*

<u>Solution</u>: Establish exact cut-off points for physical inventory counts and clearly communicate them so that your counters and accounting personnel can closely coordinate their efforts. Make sure that everyone is on the same page. In some instances, counters may choose a cut-off that is physically impossible for your accounting staff due to limitations in your accounting system. In other cases, your system may be able to make those cut offs, but your personnel may not know how to use it for anything other than end-of-the-month cut-offs.

If you want different cut-off points, speak with your vendor about acquiring a system that has all the capabilities you need, and make sure that your people receive the necessary training.

❏ *Shrink (when physical inventory count less than what your accounting system says is there.)*

<u>Solution:</u> If you have implemented the solutions I recommended previously, any remaining shrink could be due to improper markups and/or markdowns, internal product use without proper recording procedures, or inter-company transfers.

Detect weak points and areas in which errors may have occurred by flow-charting your current procedures. In many companies, the procedures that have been established are fine, but no one follows them. When that's the case, find out why the procedures are being ignored. It could be that your staff doesn't know the procedures or that they find following them too onerous.

- o Clarify to your staff why your procedures exist. Explain exactly why they have been adopted.
- o Point out to your staff how its work impacts other aspects of your business and stress the importance of everyone's following your procedures.

- o Hold your people accountable for following your procedures and specifically inform them of the consequences if they do not.
- o After you have educated your staff, periodically reinforce the importance of following your procedures with them.

❑ *Poor communication.*

<u>Solution:</u> Maintaining good inventory control requires clear communication on many levels: between your warehouse or store staff and those on the corporate level. All personnel who interact with vendors and customers must be able to communicate with them well. Understanding is the basis for good communication so check with your people to be sure that they fully understand their roles.

TIP: Automate, even when your communications are excellent; *automate whenever possible.* Automation increases efficiency because it decreases human error — and the less room for human error the better.

❑ *Antiquated inventory accounting*

<u>Solution:</u> Scanning pays for itself; in spades. Scan inventory when it comes in and then once again when it goes out at sale, even in a purely wholesale operation. Scanning, together with tightly controlled pricing, will eliminate many of your inventory problems. Add current accounting technology with compatible security technology and you'll have the battle virtually won.

> **TIP:** Many Meridian clients have told us that they experienced great success when they had random inventory counts conducted by highly skilled inventory teams. These clients report that taking inventory at various, unscheduled times throughout the month alerted them to situations that they wouldn't have caught at year-end. Plus, the randomness keeps their warehouse or store staff on their toes since they never know when the inventory team will show up.

Action items

- Understand the importance of your inventory, its value to you and its vulnerability.
- Complete the checklist above to pin point where your company could be at risk.
- Implement procedures and install systems to protect your inventory.
- Fill in the *7 Quick Fixes* Success Tracker below:

Inventory Error Checklist Cash Success Tracker

Measurable Goal	
Reward(s)	
Consequence(s)	

Action	Start Date	Target Finish	Cash Estimate	Person Responsible

Bonus Section III

REALLY SMART BANKING

So perhaps you called your banker and had some success in Quick Fix #5. Or perhaps you tried and couldn't get that quick interest rate deduction. But either result, you began to think about just how much you pay your banker each and every month. Good for you! Let's try to get some of that cash staying in your pocket.

To get ready for Bonus Chapter 22, do a quick tally of what you actually pay your bank. Your list should include:

- o Loan interest
- o Checking account fees
- o Credit card fees
- o Electronic services fees
- o Portfolio advisory fees
- o Trust service fees
- o Retirement plan fees
- o Any other fees!

When you total all that up, you'll have lots of motivation to do the work involved to reduce what you pay your financial institutions and keep more of your hard earned dollars! And, I'll show you how to leverage that information and make it work for you with banker insider secrets.

Just pick and choose from the chapters you need and go for it!

Bonus Chapter 23

WHAT ARE YOU WORTH TO YOUR BANK?

Do you know the value of your business to your bank? If not, you should. When you know how much profit your bank makes by doing business with you, you can often negotiate better loan rates, fewer fees, and smaller charges.

The profit your financial institution makes from your business depends on a number of factors including its loans to you, your deposits, and other services that the bank provides to you. Let's begin with loans.

Loans

To calculate your bank's profit on your loans, don't just look at the interest you pay because the bank incurs costs in lending money to you. Instead, find the cost that the bank pays for funds that it borrows from the Federal Reserve Bank. This cost is called the Federal Funds Rate (Fed Rate), and is published daily in most financial newspapers and on the Internet at (www.federalreserve.gov/fomc/fundsrate.htm). Then add one-quarter percent for internal servicing costs to approximate the bank's cost structure. If the Fed Rate is 3.5%, the bank's approximate cost of funds (COF) will be 3.75%.

To recap—calculate your bank's profit on your loans by:

1) Adding the Fed Rate and an internal servicing cost of 0.25 percent to find the bank's COF.
2) Subtract the bank's COF from your loan rate.
3) Multiplying the result by your loan balances.
4) Using the average loan amount outstanding over the year, the result is the bank's profit on your loans.

> **EXAMPLE:**
> - If your average loan balances are $500,000
> - Your average loan interest rates are 6%,
> - The Fed Rate is 2.5%
> - Add internal servicing costs of 0.25%
> - The calculation is: $500,000 x 3.25% or $16,250
> - Profit for your bank.

Deposits

If your money is in non-interest bearing accounts, determine your bank's profit by multiplying the amount you have on deposit by the Fed Rate. If you have $500,000 in a non-interest bearing account, that's $500,000 the bank doesn't have to borrow because it can use your money at no cost.

If your funds are in interest bearing accounts, take the Fed Rate minus your interest rate to find the bank's profit. Then factor in the fees that the bank charges on your accounts. Figure that your bank makes 50% in sheer bottom-line profit on the fees you pay. Be sure to include bank's profit on its fees before you deduct any interest credits you receive on your deposits. Also don't overlook the bank's fees on wire transactions, EFT processing, supplies and printing (deposit slips, checks, check binders, and ledgers), and other charges related to your deposit accounts.

Other Services

The final step in calculating your bank's profits is adding in the costs of other services that you purchase from your bank. These costs could be a wide range of services including investments, trusts, retirement accounts, and payroll processing.

RULE: Estimate that your bank makes a 50% profit on your total fees.

Total calculation

To find the total amount of profit that your bank earns on your business annually, add its profits on its loans to you, your deposits profit, and other services it provides to you. You may be surprised when you find how much you actually pay your bank.

TIP: After you come up with figures, use them as leverage. When you apply for your next loan, explain to your banker, "Bob, I'm really pleased that you want to make this new loan for us, but the fees are just too high. Yesterday, I took some time to calculate what we bring to your bottom line. Using the Fed Rate as a basis, I found that last year alone, you netted about $126,000 from us. So let's see if we can get rid of these fees, and strike a deal."

Also remind Bob of how long you've a loyal customer of the bank, and how many people and businesses you recommended to it.

Action items

- Determine how much profit your bank makes from its loans to your business.
- Find out the amount of profit your bank nets on your deposits.
- Calculate how much money your bank makes on the other services that it provides to your business.
- Record the actions taken in the Success Tracker below:

Bank Worth Cash Success Tracker

Measurable Goal	
Reward(s)	
Consequence(s)	

Action	Start Date	Target Finish	Cash Estimate	Person Responsible

Bonus Chapter 24

HOW TO GET YOUR BANKER TO "YES"

In recent years, many lenders have left the market, and bankruptcies have increased. So, you may have to become more aggressive in your attempts to borrow money. Most traditional banks still have plenty of money to lend, but to convince them to say "yes" can be hard. The best approach is to mount a three-pronged attack consisting of planning, preparation, and execution.

Planning

Begin by knowing precisely how much money you want to borrow, the exact amount. Don't guess. Arrive at a firm figure based on information you can document. Know what you want the additional funds for, and the terms and conditions you will accept.

In today's tight-lending climate, be ready to show lenders the reasons for your loan requests. Specifically explain to the banker exactly why your working capital line must be raised, and document your request with a simple worksheet. Create the worksheet before you apply for the loan so you know exactly how much you will need if prices in your business fluctuate.

Preparation

When you meet with a banker, present him or her with three items: a loan proposal, your company's financial information, and project information.

Prepare a formal loan proposal that includes all information that a reasonable banker will need to make a loan decision. Break down your proposal so that it provides information for each loan requested. Then for each loan, state:

1) The term requested (5 years, 10 years, etc.).
2) The specific purpose of the funds.
3) At least three different ways that you can repay each loan. Yes, three — bankers are fixated on repayment so if they see multiple options, they may feel that their money is safer.

Next, provide your company's financial information. Bankers prefer CPA prepared financial statements, but if internal statements for a small company will be acceptable. It's a good idea to include three years of profit and loss statements, balance sheets, and cash flow statements if you have them, PLUS a narrative that explains trends in those financial statements. Highlight the strong points of your business, and find ways to make the banker feel better about its weaknesses.

If you need the loan to fund a specific purchase or project, give the bank details on the purchase or project. Clearly explain how it will benefit your company, and include projections on income and expenses. If you can, show the bank that you can repay the funds even if the purchase or project doesn't pan out.

> **TIP:** Bankers are paid to be paranoid. Loan officers constantly think about risks, hidden dangers, and all the really bad stuff that could happen to you and your project. So show your banker you have thought through the risks and have alternative plans to protect the bank's interests.

When you think that your proposal is complete, give it to a non-involved third party, such as an outside board member, to review. It's easy for busy applicants to inadvertently leave out critical data, which if omitted, could cause the loan to be denied.

Execution

When you are satisfied with your loan package, call each institution. Ask if you can personally deliver your application package and explain your request. Make sure to make an appointment with a banker who has the authority to approve the loan. Don't waste your time explaining your needs to the wrong person. If asked, most bankers will be open and honest about their bank's credit process. Is it only one person who needs to approve your loan, or is it a one-up process (your request must be approved by the loan officer and their immediate superior), or committee type process? These are the three most common types of approvals, but your bank may have their own unique process, so be sure to ask so you are thoroughly prepared.

TIP: Don't rush. The old adage that "the only people bankers lend money to are those who don't need it" still applies. The less needy you appear, the stronger your chances will be of getting your loan.

Action items

- Determine exactly the amount of money you wish to borrow, how you will use it, and the terms you will accept.
- Prepare a formal loan proposal, including financial information on your company, and information about the project to be funded.
- Deliver your application package personally, and explain it to a banker who is authorized to grant the loan.
- Record the actions taken in the Success Tracker below:

Loan Package Cash Success Tracker

Measurable Goal	
Reward(s)	
Consequence(s)	

Action	Start Date	Target Finish	Cash Estimate	Person Responsible

Bonus Chapter 25

LOAN INTEREST PRICING OPTIONS

When it comes to determining what interest rate you should pay on loans, it's crucial that you understand two basic facts:

1) All loans should not be tied to the prime rate.
2) Banks may have different prime rates.

Although most of the top 10 national banks usually charge the same prime rate, many small banks have prime rates that are higher than the prime rate published in the Wall Street Journal. Before you commit to any loan, always ask the lender to disclose its current prime rate.

Bank management sets the Prime Rate. Although banks claim that Prime is the rate that they give their best borrowers, that's not always what banks actually do. Banks give their very best customers rates below their Prime Rate!

The published prime rate gives banks a very large profit. In recent years, banks have achieved record revenues because the Fed Rate (the rate at which banks borrow) was very low compared with the rates they charged their borrowers.

Alternatives to prime

For most borrowers, two alternative interest-pricing methods can be advantageous:

1) The bank's internal Cost of Funds (COF) rate.
2) London Interbank Rate (LIBOR).

Interest under the internal cost of funds approach is calculated by adding the Fed Rate plus a small spread to cover the lender's administrative costs.

Cost of Funds borrowing is considerably less than Prime Rate, and usually gives you the best and cheapest interest rate.

Another popular option is LIBOR-based borrowing which is the London Interbank rate. Again, the interest rate under this method is well below prime.

WARNING: It may also be more complex to borrow under LIBOR because loans must be in $100,000 increments for terms of 30, 60 or 90 days. If you borrow for a set period, you could be stuck for large penalties for making early payoffs.

LIBOR is also a more volatile rate than prime. For the most part, it is used as a fixed rate benchmark. If you use LIBOR for variable rate instruments, you may be in for a rocky ride and an accounting nightmare.

Other common benchmarks for loan pricing include treasury notes, Fannie Mae rates and other mortgage rates. Before you commit yourself to any loan, make sure you understand the advantages and disadvantage of any interest benchmark offered.

It's up to you

Finally, don't expect your banker to come to you with creative interest pricing methods. The compensation paid to most loan officers is based on portfolio yields. So it's in each loan officer's personal and professional best interest to get as much from you as he or she can.

Your best strategy is to simply express dissatisfaction to your banker about your rate. Let him or her clearly know that for your next loan, you expect better treatment—such as receiving interest at the Cost of Funds rate.

Action items

- Understand the Cost of Funds rate and how it's calculated.
- Understand the LIBOR rate, how it's arrived at, and its drawbacks.
- If you're not pleased with the interest rate on your loan, let your banker know.
- Record the actions taken in the *7 Quick Fixes* Success Tracker below:

Loan Pricing Cash Success Tracker

Measurable Goal	
Reward(s)	
Consequence(s)	

Action	Start Date	Target Finish	Cash Estimate	Person Responsible

Bonus Chapter 26

STRUCTURING NEW FINANCING

Before you try to finance your next project, figure out the financing structure that will best serve your company's needs. Don't simply accept all the terms that the lender proposes to you; come up with your own alternatives and negotiate. Propose creative, "out of the box" terms that will help you get a better deal.

Consider these ideas:

Loan amounts

Rather than simply financing your next new project, it may be advantageous for you to consolidate your existing loans with the new loan. This could give you larger loan, but at a lower rate because interest rates are usually cheaper on larger loans. If you need a loan for $10 million or more, you may be eligible for financing from insurance companies and lending units of the nation's top five banks.

If you get a large loan, and establish a strong repayment record, it can make your future borrowing easier. Usually, the more you repay, the more you can borrow.

Payment terms

Lenders have become more flexible and are open to granting loans on what once were unconventional terms. Negotiate to repay loans on terms that are not based on the traditional, straight-amortization formula. At a minimum, most lenders are prepared to accept interest-only payments for a limited time on start-up projects. To sweeten the deal, be willing to pay graduated increases in principal or lump sum reductions at strategic times during the life of the loan. Also consider structuring your loan repayments in cycles that mirror the ebb and flow of the cash in your business.

TIP: Never, repeat never, design a deal that calls for payments that will run longer than the life of the asset. That would be like getting a ten-year loan on a pick-up truck you'll only drive for five years. When you try to dispose of the truck, you'll owe more than it's worth. Conversely, short-term loans on long-lived assets can be brutally hard on your cash.

Interest rates

Get out of the prime rate mentality. Many lenders have granted loans at sub-prime rates because the borrowers asked for amounts pegged to LIBOR (London Interbank rates), U.S. Treasuries or the institution's internal cost of funds. Lenders differ in their ability to offer fixed or variable rates. More sophisticated lenders will offer interest rate swap mechanisms that can provide your company with best of both interest rate worlds for only a small premium. Interest rate swaps are a little complex to go into here, but worth asking about with your lender.

Collateral

When you apply for loans, try to be creative by offering to put up no collateral or collateral that is not in any way involved in the project funded by the loan. For example, I've had clients provide trucks as collateral for new real estate development projects.

Learn each lender's comfort zone with collateral, and offer only what you don't mind tying up for the length of the loan, which ideally, will also help you get the cheapest loan. Some lenders accept "Negative Pledge" collateral. That means that the lender does not take any actual collateral, but your company promises not to allow any other lenders to place a lien on its property.

Loan Agreement Covenants

Covenants is a fancy banking term for requirements. Know the loan terms you can live with and what you can't. Then, clearly communicate that information to lenders when you submit your loan proposal. Ask potential lenders to explain to you their typical requirements before you apply for a loan. The information that you receive may help you eliminate a few lenders from your list, which can save you considerable time and expense. Covenants are serious stuff. A banker can force you to pay a loan early if you violate promised financial ratios in your loan covenants.

Action items

- When you apply for new loans, consider consolidating them with your existing loans if you can lower your rates.
- Negotiate nonstandard terms and interest rates.
- Determine what loan terms you will accept and inform potential lenders of them.
- Record the actions taken in the Success Tracker:

Loan Structuring Cash Success Tracker

Measurable Goal	
Reward(s)	
Consequence(s)	

Action	Start Date	Target Finish	Cash Estimate	Person Responsible

Bonus Chapter 27

HOW TO KEEP YOUR BANKER HAPPY

Alternative lenders now look more like revolving doors than viable financing options, so it's a good time to keep traditional bankers happy. Commercial banks still give the most business loans despite the intermittent splashes made by other types of lenders.

If you want to continually get the lowest lending rates, keep your banker happy. Here are seven rules to follow:

1. Keep your banker informed on industry trends. As part of his or her job, your banker is charged with understanding industry risk. Unfortunately, the press likes to sensationalize negatives such as supply problems, bankruptcies, fraud, illegal activities, and the like. Even if your industry is healthy and growing, your banker may not get that impression from the media. So, educate him or her.

Become a PR person for your industry. Combat negativity by regularly mailing and faxing your banker positive and accurate data on your industry as you come across it. That information could help your banker's career by providing him or her with important information that he or she might otherwise never learn.

2. Educate your banker on your industry and your company. Teach your banker about terms, methods, and conditions that are specific to or critical to your industry. Tell him or her about the best, most vital industry publications, newsletters, Web sites, and blogs. Teach him or her how to think and to talk like an industry insider.

TIP: Inform your banker of your businesses' major new accounts, new sites, awards, sponsorships, and civic and charitable efforts. Send him or her copies of articles about you or your business and alert him or her before your media appearances. When bad news regarding your company is about to break, beat others to the punch. Immediately tell your banker yourself. Never let your banker first learn negative news through the grapevine.

3. Make timely submissions. Never be late, either for appointments or with your responsibilities. Promptness equates to reliability, and bankers place a high premium on reliability.

When you are obligated to submit payments, financial statements, documents, receivables aging and listings, or anything else, get it to your banker before it's due.

4. Pick up the tab. Invite your banker to lunch and pay. Personally give him or her a tour of sites or projects that his or her bank funded. Ask your banker to your business celebrations, and try to make him or her fell like a part of your business family.

Most bankers can name on one hand the customers who ever bought them lunch. It's a small gesture, but one bankers never forget. Treat your banker as you would any other important business contact; be gracious and show your appreciation. Always work to build and maintain a strong good personal relationship with your banker.

5. Send referrals. Like you, your banker is in business and is always looking for new customers. When you hear someone grumbling about his or her existing financing or new projects, recommend your banker. Or let your banker know so he or she can call the prospect.

TIP: Tell your banker what he or she could do to attract more business from companies in your industry. Point out when better deals or terms are being offered by other lenders so that your banker can ask for the authority to match or top them.

6. Remember bankers are paid to think "worst case." Try to think like your banker. Anticipate the risks that might concern your banker and prepare address and minimize them. As a businessperson, you by definition are a risk-taker, but your banker is risk-averse; he or she always will worry about the downside risks. Address those worries instead of pretending that they don't exist.

When you give bankers projections, be ultra conservative, as a banker would. When you explain how you plan to pay back a loan, give your banker alternative ways that you could pay should your first repayment option go dry. For bankers, three repayment alternatives seem to be the magic number.

7. Understand your bank's process and politics. Try to look at everything involved in your loan application from your banker's perspective. Do background research. Find out what loans the bank has been granting and the terms it obtained. Learn what risks the bank refuses to fund. Also obtain information about conditions at the bank, if it is doing well, its internal politics, and the impact of competitive lenders.

If you understand your banker's challenges, you can shape your application to get the most favorable response. If you can take steps that make your banker look good, sooner or later, somewhere down the line, your banker may help you, and borrowing money can become easier.

Action items

- Send your banker positive and accurate data on your business and your industry as you come across it.
- Be prompt and never be late for your appointments or submissions.
- Try to think like your banker—anticipate and prepare to address his or her probable concerns.
- Record the actions taken in the Success Tracker below:

Banker Relationship Cash Success Tracker

Measurable Goal	
Reward(s)	
Consequence(s)	

Action	Start Date	Target Finish	Cash Estimate	Person Responsible

Bonus Chapter 28

HELP FOR TAPPED OUT BANK CREDIT LINES

At Meridian, we have been receiving a record number of SOS's from folks who maxed out their credit and still need more working capital. If you find yourself in the same bind, here's what to do plus some tips on how you can avoid getting into these money crunches in the future.

Prepare to fess up to your banker

If you used your credit line to buy a bunch of fixed assets, convert (term out) the portion of your line that you inadvertently used to buy assets to a term loan with fixed payout. Here's how you should proceed:

- Dig up all your receipts to find out exactly how much of your credit line was used to buy equipment, vehicles, building improvements, land, and so forth.
- Be detailed and precise because you'll be showing them to your banker.
- Collect all your receipts for a base year, and then work back as many as three years until you compile a meaningful dollar total.
- Remember that most bankers only fund about 75% of your costs, especially since a year or two may have passed since you made your purchases.

How much working capital will you need?

To determine the size of the credit line you will need, estimate the highest amount of receivables you expect to take in this year. Add in the highest amount of inventory you will carry and deduct the least amount of trade payables you will incur. Round off your total to the nearest $100,000 increment. The amount you arrive at will be the size of the credit line you will need after you rid yourself of your asset purchases.

EXAMPLE:

Your current line	$1,500,000
Amount used to buy assets	$900,000
Estimated max receivables	$2,200,000
Estimated max inventory	$400,000
Estimated min payables	$1,400,000

Assume that your $1,500,000 line is fully drawn, and the bank agrees to term out 75% of the $900,000 that you used to buy assets or $675,000.

On the basis of your forecast of $2.2 million in receivables plus $400,000 inventory, minus $1,400,000 trade payables, you will need a $1,200,000 line of credit. If you get that line, but you've already have borrowed some money, let's say $825,000 for this example, you would then have an additional $375,000 in your new line that you could borrow.

Estimate capital asset purchases

Before you see your banker, estimate how much you will need to purchase in capital assets over the next year so you can request a separate line of credit for those needs. An asset-purchase line will prevent you from depleting your working-capital line again, and it will preserve your original line for its intended function.

Structure your asset-purchase line so that just before the end of your fiscal year, any balances that exist on the line will automatically convert to a term loan, which will help keep your current ratio (current assets divided by current liabilities) within acceptable bank and supplier preferred ranges.

EXAMPLE: You request a $400,000 credit line to meet your upcoming needs. On December 31, the end of your fiscal year, you owe $376,000, which is then converted to a five-year term loan. On your year-end financials, only one-fifth of the loan amount is a current liability, not 100% as it would have been had you used your working-capital line for the purpose.

Present your request

Now you are ready to ask your banker to restructure your debt. You should:

- Term out $675,000 to a five-year note that is supported by $900,000 worth of purchase invoices.
- Adjust your working capital line to $1,200,000.
- Open a new $400,000 asset-purchase line. For this line, funding at 75% of the invoice price will be pre-approved. When you make a purchase, all you have to do is fax the invoice to the bank and it will immediately place 75% of the invoice price in your checking account.

TIP: To support your restructuring request, give the banker up-to-date financial statements and volume reports that document your company's growing profitably. If you're in a non-profitable period, bring projections showing how and when you will return to profitability. If personal guarantees are involved with company debt, also submit updated personal financial statements.

It never hurts to be the bearer of good news. So also show your banker pictures of your new sites, grand openings, employee functions, new Web sites, awards, and favorable press on your company to build his or her confidence in you.

Under your new debt structure, your bank's financial commitment to you will total $2,275,000, which is a $775,000 increase over its prior $1,500,000 commitment. If your bank is reluctant to restructure your debt, it may be time to look for another lender. Fortunately, the lending environment is still very competitive, and you will probably find plenty folks that want your business.

Two additional guidelines

As you work on the details of your new loan structure, keep two items in mind.

1) Your asset-purchase line and revolving-credit line should have the same variable interest rate. You may want a fixed rate for the asset term-out loan plus have the option of a fixed rate when the asset-purchase line converts into a fixed-term loan.

2) If your company's balance sheet shows strong profits, you may be able to lower your borrowing rates by pegging the interest you'll be charged to LIBOR rather than prime.

Action items

- Term out the portion of your credit line that you used to buy fixed buy assets.
- Calculate the exact amount of the credit line you need.
- Prepare documentation that will convince your banker to restructure your debt.
- Record the actions taken in the *7 Quick Fixes* Success Tracker below:

Credit Line Cash Success Tracker

Measurable Goal	
Reward(s)	
Consequence(s)	

Action	Start Date	Target Finish	Cash Estimate	Person Responsible

Bonus Chapter 29

WHEN TO SWITCH BANKS

Face it — it's not fun to change banks, and your bank may know and take advantage of that fact. However, at certain times and under some conditions, moving your business may make great sense, and you should seriously consider going with another bank.

In recent years, the banking climate has changed. In many cases, it's become more competitive so businesses may have more options regarding which banks to deal with and the types and costs of services that they can receive. Many banks have also become more flexible, more customer focused, and more eager to please.

To see if you should switch banks, answer the following 10 questions. Circle either T, for true, or F, for false, for each question. Then review your answers; they will help you decide if you should stay put or endure the pain of change.

Banking test

T   F   My bank is generally responsive to my business needs and requests.

T   F   When my business needs need a loan, my bank provides a specific list of the information it needs to evaluate the request. The information the bank requests is reasonable and easy to provide.

T   F   My bank's rates and fees are competitive for the area.

T   F   Since my business deposits substantial amounts with the bank, it gives us preferred checking account fees and services.

T F   My bank has my business checking account, line of credit, and overnight investment accounts automatically linked so we don't have to manage our daily cash flow.

T F   My bank has or will help us set-up EFT system to collect our customer accounts.

T F   My business can move money to or from any of our accounts without leaving our office by using a PC link to the bank.

T F   My bank informs us in a timely manner of new, beneficial products and services as they become available.

T F   My bank offers high-yielding portfolios for our excess cash.

T F   My bank makes us feel like a valued customer.

Scoring

Add up how many questions you answered "true." Then use the key below to see if it's time to switch.

10: Wow. Tell me the name of your bank. You're fortunate, indeed.

7 - 9: Stay put. Overall, you're doing well. Discuss the questions that were answered "false" with your bank representative.

5 - 6: Try to negotiate to get better service. Give the bank the chance to improve, but if it won't yield, consider moving.

Less than 5: It's time to go out to bid. You deserve better treatment. Sometimes, the fact that your bank knows you are prepared to move and bid will force them to shape up. On the other hand, when you review other proposals, it may be in your businesses' best interest to switch banks.

TIP: When you consider everything—interest, fees, terms, services, and time, you will find that your banking relationship is very important to your company's bottom-line. Let the idea of extra profit keep you motivated while you work to optimize your banking.

Action items

- Take the banking test and answer all the questions.
- Discuss all of the questions that you answered "false" with your banker to try to get improved service.
- If you answer at least half of the questions "false," investigate whether you could receive better service from other banks.
- Record the actions taken in the Success Tracker:

Bank Switch Score Cash Success Tracker

Measurable Goal	
Reward(s)	
Consequence(s)	

Action	Start Date	Target Finish	Cash Estimate	Person Responsible

Bonus Chapter 30

BETTER-BANKING CHECKLIST

Since banking and financing can be so crucial to your business, let's recap some of the information that I covered in this Bonus section to stress major points. A few of the items below were touched on lightly, so this checklist provides another chance for me to impress their value to you.

> **TIP:** Remember that you may have more clout with bankers and financiers than you realize. So review this checklist and try flexing a little muscle by implementing some of the following strategic moves. They could substantially lower your cost of doing business and position you for greater success.

- ☐ ***Know your value.*** Determine the value of your business to your bank. Specifically calculate how much money your bank makes as a result of its loans to you, your deposits, what you pay for its other services, and business that referred to the bank. When you come up with an amount, visit your banker and negotiate better loan rates, fewer fees, and smaller charges.

- ☐ ***Keep your banker happy.*** Make your banker your friend and treat him or her as your unofficial partner. Educate your banker about your business and your industry. Apprise him or her about developments in your company. Don't let your banker hear about problems from anyone else.

  Submit payments, applications, and anything else on time and make sure that it's accurate and complete. Occasionally, take your banker to lunch and pick up the tab. Send referrals, and think like your banker by understanding and addressing the bank's concerns—especially about possible risks.

- ☐ ***Pay down working capital lines.*** Install a system that automatic pays down your working capital lines. If, at the end of any business day, you have cash in your checking account, your automatic system should apply it to your line of credit, which will decrease the amount of interest you owe. Most banks now offer this service and can help you put it in place. If your bank does not, ask your loan officer to show a loan clerk how to do this function every day.

- **Consolidate loans.** Bundle all your small notes payable into one, low-cost loan. By borrowing a larger amount of money in one loan, you can save the bank administrative costs. Usually, consolidating your debts will enable you to lower your interest rate by one-half point.

- **Learn financing fundamentals.** Familiarize yourself with different types of loans and loan structures. Understand down payments, types of interest, amortization, personal guarantees, collateral, and other requirements.

- **Get low-cost loans.** Ask for your loans to be set at the LIBOR (London Interbank) rate, or Cost of Funds rate, which are usually lower than the prime-based interest rates that most banks charge. LIBOR rates run for 30, 60 or 90-day terms, and can be tracked in the Wall Street Journal.

  Rarely do you see banks quoting rates at "Prime minus __%," but you will see offers for "LIBOR plus." Banks set the prime rates and tell their customers that it's the rate they give their best borrowers, but that's not always true. Show bankers that you're savvy by requesting LIBOR pegged rates, which are typically below prime.

- **Request preferential checking account fees.** Banks charge fees on various checking account transactions such as deposits, wires transfers, checks, and printing, to name a few. If your business regularly runs large amounts through your accounts, it provides your bank with money that it can access at no change. In exchange for your business, request your bank give you reduced prices on your checking account fees. When you negotiate, safely assume your bank builds has at least a 50% profit into all of its fees.

- **Keep your eggs in one basket.** When most of your loans and deposits are with one institution, not spread around, you usually get the best rates.

Loyalty counts, but it can also make you vulnerable if you don't get what you request from your bank, if it takes your business for granted, or sours on your industry, as banks often do.

So always keep at least one other bank in the wings. Consider placing smaller accounts with it, which could facilitate your decision to switch. Always keep abreast of conditions in the banking industry; know the going rates and terms. Try to have other institutions knocking at your door, and breathlessly seeking your business.

☐ ***Periodically bid out your needs.*** Even though loyalty pays, blind loyalty is foolish, and often quite expensive. Plus, change can be good. It can introduce you to visionary thinkers, new contacts, and new, unique, and more beneficial systems and procedures.

Keep your bank on its toes and make sure to get the best deals, by seeking competitive bids on your banking business every three years. Approach banks as you would any other vendor; on the value they will provide to you. Learn what rates and terms and rates you can receive, and see if you bank will meet or beat them.

Action items

- Periodically review the better-banking checklist, and think about each item.
- Identify items on the better-banking checklist that you are not using to your advantage.
- Take specific steps to use or position your business to use the items on the better-banking checklist.
- Record actions taken in Success Tracker below:

Banking Checklist Cash Success Tracker

Measurable Goal	
Reward(s)	
Consequence(s)	

Action	Start Date	Target Finish	Cash Estimate	Person Responsible

Bonus Section IV

MARKETING ON STEROIDS

One of the most fun things to do in business is to create a rush of cash inflow. To position your company for that rush, takes a hard look at your customers, your products, and new possibilities. This means getting your head up and looking at the horizon. Sometimes we are so busy working in our existing business, that we miss out on tremendous opportunities.

In this section, you'll:

- Discover how to determine which customers make you the most money
- Pinpoint customers that are literally sucking the cash out of your business and get rid of them.
- Create new sources of cash

To get you in the learning frame of mind, I want to share some insight I gained with you. Heating oil distributors often are classic examples of companies missing huge cash opportunities. When the winter is cold and prices are favorable, these owners love their businesses. Give them a warm winter with unanticipated price swings, and all I'd hear was how bad it was! I couldn't help but think in my early days, if it's this bad, why do you still do it?

But, I as the years went on, I noticed I had other clients with substantial heating oil sales who were profitable no matter the temperature or price. What they had done was strategically position their companies so heating oil didn't make or break them. They could have a bad season and still make a dandy profit. How? With counter cyclical products (such as air conditioning or pool services) or with non-seasonal products (such as retail gas station fuel supply).

More recently, in a non-heating fuel situation, I watched two petro marketers whose businesses centered on contractors make opposite decisions when contractors started down-sliding. One guy did nothing and is barely hanging on, while the other created an enormous gush of cash inflow by mastering another fuel market sector (mobile refueling).

By using the techniques in this Bonus section, you can create that gush of cash you need and deserve!

> **Encouragement:** Did you know that God's first verb in the Bible was create? Genesis 1:1 says "In the beginning, God created" and later goes on to say in verse 26 that man was created in His own image. Based on this scripture, I've come to fully believe that you and I are at our best self when we are creating. Therefore, I pray that as you read this Bonus Section, God will multiply your creativity to produce goods and services with such high value to the marketplace that you will see huge inflows of cash as a result.

Bonus Chapter 31

HOW TO KEEP PROFITABLE CUSTOMERS (AND DUMP THE REST!)

Here's a hard statistical fact: 20% of any business' customers account for 80% of their profits. Whether you are in the wholesale, retail, or service sectors, 20% of your customers are great, 60% are average, and 20% are not so great—translation: you may actually lose money on them. To operate profitably, identify your best customers and use that knowledge to increase your profits.

To tackle this challenge, classify all of your customers into A-B-C rankings.

A = Your best customers in terms of bottom-line profit.
B = Your average customers.
C = Customers you do not profit from or lose money on.

Wholesalers

If you're a wholesaler, you make good profit margins with your A customers. You also receive prompt payment and provide normal deliveries. With C customers, you have low margins, are paid late, and have delivery difficulties. B customers are all those that fall anywhere between A and C.

Everyone in your organization must know which of your customers are in groups A and C, and they should give your A customers preferential treatment. It's crucial for your people to know which customers belong in each group, because C customers typically call frequently and demand immediate service. Dispatchers will often authorize faster deliveries to C customers who pester them just to get them off their backs. However, in the process, loads to your A customers may be bumped.

C customers also tend to hound you for extras and special service requests. They befriend your staff while your big-dollar A customers, who rarely request extras or complain, are shunted off like a second-class accounts.

TIP: If you ignore your A customer, they can become easy targets for your competitors. If rivals even vaguely sense an opening, they will strike like lightning—fast and powerfully. They will approach your customers and ask, "When's the last time you saw your rep?" or "What have they done for you lately?" To get your customers' business, your competitors will cut their prices and offer them a "better" deal. So make sure each of your A accounts is treated with the extra attention and service it deserves.

Reevaluate all of your C customers. First, determine if each is worth keeping. If you're losing money on an account after you factor in service, either (1) raise your margins or (2) charge fees that will put each account in the black. If these changes drive C-level accounts to your competitors, so be it. In fact, try to find ways to send all your problems to your competitors; better that they lose money on marginal customers than you.

Try to elevate your B customers to the A level. Explore whether you can sell them more products, make higher profits, or get them to pay you more promptly. Contact them to find what more you could provide. No matter what you do, some B customers will always stay at their present level, which is OK. Just make sure you don't allow them to drop to Cs.

Retailers

If you operate a retail business, profile your customers. Use your register data to categorize them in the A-B-C groups I recommended for wholesalers. When you do, you'll find that to 20-80% rule holds true: your A customers produce 80% of your gross profits. Cultivate your A customers, and market directly to them to increase your sales and profits.

Grocery chains have loyalty card programs to identify customer levels. In these programs, customers are given a card that the chains use to keep track of every dime each "club member" spends, and the precise products he or she buys. Although you may not have the technology or funds to establish a loyalty program, here's how to accomplish the same results.

First, identify how much money your A-list customers spend. Gather all your store customer transaction data, dump it into a spreadsheet, sort it according to the highest sales dollars to the lowest, and then where the line for the top 20% individual customer transaction falls.

EXAMPLE:

If you find that the average ticket size for your A-category customers is $20.00:

Have your cashiers ask each customer who spends $20 or more to fill out a quick survey. Immediately give each customer that completes the survey a coupon for a free item, such as a fountain drink, a future discount, or some other item. Ask these questions in the survey:

1) How frequently do you shop at our store? Daily, more than once per week, weekly, etc.
2) What is your home zip code?
3) Check the reasons why you shop at our store. Provide multiple-choice answers that will be easy for them to complete.
4) What did you buy today?
5) If you could change one thing about this store, what would it be?
6) What product or service would you like to buy that we are missing?

Use the information you receive from the survey to cater to your A customers and provide the products they want. Your top customers' zip codes, will inform you where they live so you can develop a target marketing programs in those areas to create more A-level customers.

Also take a hard look at your bottom 20% customers, those on your C list, to see what they're buying. If your C-group customers are the only ones buying certain products, consider getting rid of those items.

Action items

- Classify all of your customers into A-B-C rankings, with A being your best customers and C being your worst.
- Provide preferential treatment to your A-list customers.
- Determine if it pays to keep your C-level customers and/or items they buy.
- Record the actions taken in the Success Tracker:

ABC Customer Cash Success Tracker

Measurable Goal	
Reward(s)	
Consequence(s)	

Action	Start Date	Target Finish	Cash Estimate	Person Responsible

Bonus Chapter 32

TARGET MARKETING

Laser Focus Produces More Cash and Profits

Why concern yourself with target marketing? The answer is two simple words – CASH and PROFIT!

By accurately defining a specific target market and then fully penetrating that market, your business is sure to make more money. Target marketing works with laser beam precision whether you have a wholesale, retail or a service business. It will turn your company's most promotable competitive edge into a powerful marketing message delivered directly to the right prospects.

A business that fails to define a target market, and attempts to sell to the whole universe, will never achieve maximum cash and profits. Those that try don't understand that every product and service appeals more strongly to a certain definable group. Target marketing is all about defining that group. It requires you to:

- Identify who you want as your customer (regardless of who is buying from you now) and
- Provide the products and services they most desire and need.

Target marketing boosts your cash and profit by narrowing your focus to only the "right" prospects — so you don't waste your time and resources. At the same time, it reduces your promotion and operating costs and maximizes your profits.

Identify possible choices

Choices abound for your target market(s). You can segregate possible pools using specific criteria depending on your company's focus. For example, retail, wholesale or service. If you have a wholesale business, you can use industry classification to segregate potential target markets through either U.S. government's Standard Industry Classifications, or simply using your local yellow pages to identify industry categories of potential buyers.

If you operate a retail business, segregate your target market by demographic factors such as age group, socio-economic level, occupation, geography, etc. Use any and every breakdown that makes sense to you. Look beyond your unit's neighborhood demographics to include anyone who might be driving by. Using this data, make a list of the types of customers you could potentially serve or sell to. Don't limit your thinking. You are in the stage where more is better, so don't be satisfied with what you come up with on your first try.

Marketing guru Dan Kennedy tells the story of a man who sold product distributorships using the phone book white pages, which was an expensive and incredibly inefficient way to reach the right market. He finally took a hard look at his actual customers and saw that they were mostly fortyish men with out-of-style crew cuts.

He realized that stubborn individualists, men prone to crew-cuts, were exactly his target market and immediately changed his marketing plan to send recruiters out to barber shops. The result? Phenomenal success! The moral to the story: *Don't limit yourself to conventional thinking when it comes to target markets.*

If you own a service business, your target market segmentation will depend on your end customer. If your end customers are businesses, use SIC codes or yellow pages. If they are consumers, use demographics similar to a retailer. If both, use both sets of data.

Profit potential

Take your list of potential target market categories and estimate the gross profit potential to your company over the next year for each market. Yes, this takes some guesswork, but you'll usually be reasonably accurate just using a little common sense and past customer sales history.

EXAMPLE:

One of my clients identified senior citizens, working professionals, and teenagers as three possible target markets for their store. Based upon its current sales trends, it estimated the weekly gross profit from one typical individual from each group. Then it estimated how many of those folks would visit its store in a week under ideal circumstances (including clever advertising). The figures they came up with gave my client the gross profit potential for each segment.

Target market compatibility

In some instances, there may be several good target markets, but they aren't all compatible and some could downright clash. Continuing with our scenario from the example above, let's say you own a retail location and decided that white-collar workers who travel to a business park located a mile past your store is your top target. However, your store is located right smack in the middle of a retirement community, but there is also a junior high school one-half block away. Thinking logically about product needs for each of these three possible target markets, you can see how the working professionals and seniors would buy similar products such as gourmet coffees and lotto tickets, but not the teens. The teens would require an entire separate product offering. In addition, a large teen crowd might prevent the older age groups from frequenting your store. Therefore, you conclude your primary market should be the drive-by white-collar professionals, with a compatible secondary market of neighborhood seniors, and decide to exclude the incompatible teen market.

Products

Carry only those products your target group customers love; design your product offering to match your target groups' needs. By focusing all your creative product energy on your target market(s), you will either intuitively know exactly what products and services to offer or can verify through surveys and publicly available market research. This also means you may need to dump some existing products (like you dumped customers in Chapter 30!) that aren't a fit for your target market.

Promotion

To tailor and deliver the right promotional message to your target group(s), think like they do! What discount or promotion will appeal to your target customer? With target marketing, you intimately know your desired customer so you can identify exactly what will entice those customers to buy more from you. For instance, in the convenience store industry, a professional or senior customer would NOT be enticed by a low priced gallon of milk, but they might come in droves for a coffee club, or daily specialty coffee that would skyrocket sales.

Target market psychology works for the wholesale segment as well. Since you want to penetrate a specific industry, you just need to find out what would get them to buy from you. For example, it might be industry-specific technical expertise. Therefore, hiring salespersons from your target industries who know the industry could be your ticket to exponential sales.

Measure results

Things don't always go as we plan, so check your actual results against your beginning forecast. Measuring results, including market penetration will help you fine-tune your promotions and the inevitable market changes you detect will help you adjust the markets that you target as you go along. If you keep your laser sharp focus, and measure your results, you'll know exactly when to move.

Action Items

- Identify possible target pools — brainstorm a long list of possibilities.
- Identify your top few targets by estimating the profits potential for each segment.
- Check product offerings against your target markets' wants and needs — make adjustments when necessary.
- Develop and execute on enticing promotions
- Measure results and be prepared to respond appropriately, especially to market changes.
- Record the actions taken in the Success Tracker

Target Marketing Cash Success Tracker

Measurable Goal	
Reward(s)	
Consequence(s)	

Action	Start Date	Target Finish	Cash Estimate	Person Responsible

Chapter 33

HIT THE EMOTIONAL HOT BUTTON (AND WATCH NEW CASH ROLL IN!)

Even if you have a highly defined target market (see Chapter 31), your competitors will want to get in on your action. They will try to sell to those exact same targets. So you MUST stand out from the crowd. Stand out by:

- Creating an outrageously different marketing message than your competitors
- Pressing your target customers' emotional hot buttons
- Consistently reaching your targets over and over and over again or
- Ideally, a combination of all three!

You have only to watch a Super Bowl to see just how outrageous marketing messages can become. Or read Seth Godin's *Purple Cow* for a great overview about standing out from the crowd. Lots of marketing books have been written about uniqueness so I won't replicate that information here. Instead, I want you to focus on the other two critical keys that will give you more cash from your marketing.

Emotional Appeal Sells

Does your current marketing message have emotional impact on your target customer? To find out, ask the "So what" question as master marketer, Jay Conrad Levinson, suggests. Other than just grabbing attention, a powerful marketing message needs to answer, "So what does that mean" from your target customer's point of view. You must get in that customer's head!

EXAMPLE: A toothpaste ad claims to get your teeth really white. If we apply the "So what" question to getting teeth white, let's look at what the responses might be depending on the target market:

- Adult Singles: I'll be more attractive to the opposite sex, which means no more lonely Saturday nights.
- Teens: My tan will look darker, I'll be sexier and so I'll definitely have my preferred prom date.
- Mature married people: No one will know I smoke.

See how different messages must be for different targets. The "So what" question gets you to the emotional hook of your product of service.

Business owners often mistakenly assume that buying is a rational process, especially in selling business to business. Nothing could be further from the truth! There is nothing rational about buying behavior. And in fact, businesses don't buy. People buy. And they buy to alleviate pain (the strongest motivator) or to create pleasure. Tap into your buyers' emotions, join the conversation that is already going on in their heads, and you will create streams of new cash for your business.

Touchpoint Frequency

Now let's talk about how often your prospects need to see your message. Do you ever see the same TV commercial over and over the same night? That's smart marketing, it drives home the message and you can do the same thing. You can even do it on a shoestring budget.

Your target customer is being bombarded daily with advertising on the radio, TV, mail, email, magazines, billboards, you name it. Because we've become such an advertising rich society, your customer is an expert at ignoring all these messages, including yours. And the tighter your budget, the less likely it is that they will see your ads!

But an interesting thing happens once an emotionally powerful, on target, message is delivered over and over and over again. All of a sudden, after seeing that message for the 9th or 10th, or 12th or 20th time…BINGO! Your message gets through. Now why does this happen? Well, some marketing gurus say it may be timing – you finally reached your prospects at the point when they need your product and are ready to buy. Other marketing experts say that frequency builds trust, and trust facilitates buying.

I'm not sure which is right, or if both are right, but no matter what advertising medium you choose, think about frequency. The latest research shows that weekly frequency far outweighs monthly messages. Does that mean that daily outpaces weekly, or that several times in one night outpaces once per day? Not necessarily. Frequency can be taken to an annoying level and drive buyers away, so test to find the right frequency for your targets. Diminishing returns and negative customer feedback are warning signs of annoyance.

Don't always sell

Since you want frequent touch points, but you don't want to annoy your customer, think about running a message that has no sales pitch! While it may seem counterintuitive, at first, the most powerful marketing strategy may be to strictly provide information. Today's buyers are so swamped with sales messages that they may appreciate helpful, non-sales tips or education. As your target market begins to see you as "The Expert", they will be more inclined to buy from you.

EXAMPLE: A marketing software company sent me weekly emails on how to improve my marketing without any product pitches. After a bunch of really great, information-rich emails, it dawned on me these guys really knew their stuff! So, I realized their software could free up my time, plus make sure my prospects were getting frequent touches without me having to do anything (it's all automated). I purchased!

Using marketing in an information-rich, non-sales way positions you as an expert in your customers' minds. Later, if and when you send a sales message that has the "So What" question answered, they will trust you and buy.

Test and Measure

Marketing must have Return on Investment. Even so-called "free" email marketing takes time and time is money. As you test and execute your new marketing strategies, keep careful records on response rates and on who your buyers are. Always look to improve your best!

Action Items

- Create and test at least one unique marketing message that hits your target market's emotional hot buttons.
- Test a "non-sales" information-based marketing strategy that positions your company as the expert with a one portion of your target market.
- Keep accurate data on money and time spent, responses and results.
- Record the actions taken in the Success Tracker

Emotional Hot Button Cash Success Tracker

Measurable Goal	
Reward(s)	
Consequence(s)	

Action	Start Date	Target Finish	Cash Estimate	Person Responsible

Betsi Bixby and her company Meridian Associates, Inc. currently assist over 3,500 of this country's privately held, family-led petroleum companies increase cash flow and profits through education, strategic planning facilitation, merger mediation, business valuation and advisory services. Her message is one of executable steps and core competencies that every business owner or manager needs to know.

Betsi has been the most widely read cash flow expert in the petroleum industry, where pennies not dollars dictate success, for over two decades. Through her Money Matters column published by the Petroleum Marketers Association of America (PMAA) and many state and regional petroleum, convenience store, and propane associations, years of publishing her newsletter *The Meridian Financial Advantage*, and now her PetroAnswers resource website, Betsi clarifies and simplifies complicated subjects into concrete step-by-step processes that dramatically impact company performance and profits.

A financial sharp shooter, Betsi is well known for the value she brings to businesses and the families that own them. By customer demand, Betsi began Meridian's highly acclaimed Valuation and Advisory division in late 1999. Betsi and Meridian quickly earned a reputation for accurate market valuations and have continued to achieve great success facilitating highly confidential sales of family-owned companies.

Betsi Bixby is also well-known by major petroleum refiners, conducting training each year for the major gasoline brands. Betsi's background includes an MBA in Finance and serving as Vice President of Commercial Lending for a regional bank. She captivates convention audiences throughout the U.S. with her hard-hitting, practical key note addresses and workshops.

In 2011, Betsi became a founding member of the John Maxwell Team, intensely studying John C, Maxwell and his leadership principles based on his premise that "Everything rises and falls on leadership." Betsi traveled with The John Maxwell Team to Guatemala and Paraguay facilitating leadership round-tables. She and her team coach family business CEOs and their executive teams to new levels of personal and professional success.

In May 2015, Betsi signed a book publishing deal with noted Chicken Soup author Jack Canfield for Soul of Success Vol 2, where the world's leading entrepreneurs and professionals reveal their core strategies for getting to the heart of health, wealth and success. After hitting the Best Seller's list both nationally and internationally at it's debut September 2015, Betsi was given the Quilly Award by the National Academy of Best-Selling Authors.

Also in October 2016, Betsi joined a select group of entrepreneurs from around the world to co-write the book titled, *Professional Performance 360 Special Edition: Success.*

On the day of release, *Professional Performance 360 Special Edition: Success* reached Amazon best-seller status. Betsi contributed *"Ten Steps to Move the Family Company from Business to Legacy."*

With Christ-centered personal ethics, Betsi strives to be a blessing to her customers, her employees and the family businesses she loves. Residing in Weatherford, Texas where she enjoys a ranching lifestyle, complete with cattle and horses, her equestrian pursuits include a top three national ranking by The American Competitive Trail Horse Association. In 2011, she co-founded **Freedom Horses,** a non-profit 501 (c)3 organization that links survivors of domestic violence with volunteer horse owners to build courage, compassion and confidence. Betsi is former Chairman of the Tucson YMCA, former President of Greater Tucson Leadership, and former President of Soroptimist International of Tucson. Betsi considers her greatest accomplishment to be her daughter Sheila, who achieved a Masters in Behavioral Health Counseling and now resides in Austin.

GET MORE AT

WWW.7QUICKFIXESBOOK.COM

www.ingramcontent.com/pod-product-compliance
Lightning Source LLC
Chambersburg PA
CBHW071759200526
45167CB00017B/484